Hellfire Pass

Vittorio Rossi

HELLFIRE PASS

A Carpenter's Trilogy
A Chronicle in Three Plays
Part One

Talonbooks
Vancouver

Talonbooks
P.O. Box 2076, Vancouver, British Columbia, Canada V6B 3S3
www.talonbooks.com

Typeset in New Baskerville and printed and bound in Canada.

First Printing: 2007

The publisher gratefully acknowledges the financial support of the Canada Council for the Arts; the Government of Canada through the Book Publishing Industry Development Program; and the Province of British Columbia through the British Columbia Arts Council and the Book Publishing Tax Credit for our publishing activities.

Library and Archives Canada Cataloguing in Publication

Rossi, Vittorio, 1961–

    Hellfire pass : a carpenter's trilogy : a chronicle in three plays, part one / Vittorio Rossi.

ISBN 978-0-88922-564-0

    I. Title.

PS8585.O8425H44 2007   C812'.54   C2006-906485-7

In loving memory of my father

Hellfire Pass was first produced by Centaur Theatre Company in Montréal, Quebec. Its premiere took place on February 2, 2006 with the following cast:

SILVIO .... Richard Zeppieri
EDUARDO .... Harry Standjofski
ANGELINA .... Lally Cadeau
EDDIE .... Julian Tassielli
IDA .... Tara Nicodemo
BOBBY .... Mark Camacho
RITA .... Lauren Spring

Director: Gordon McCall
Set design: John Dinning
Costume design: Susana Vera
Lighting design: Luc Prairie
Production manager: Howard Mendelsohn
General manager: Charles Childs
Stage manager: Chris Hidalgo
Assistant stage manager: Sarah Bustard

Characters

SILVIO ROSATO, *36, a carpenter and a decorated World War II veteran.*

EDUARDO ROSATO, *60, Silvio's father, an aluminum plant manager.*

ANGELINA ROSATO, *58, Eduardo's wife.*

EDDIE ROSATO, JR., *32, Silvio's half-brother, a salesman.*

IDA ROSATO, *35, Silvio's half-sister.*

BOBBY TARDELLI, *37, Ida's husband, a mechanic, an Italian-American.*

RITA TESTA, *22, Silvio's friend, a student.*

Place

Chicago, Illinois.

Time

Autumn, 1956.

ACT ONE

Scene One: Late morning.

Scene Two: Early that afternoon.

Scene Three: Later that night.

ACT TWO

Scene One: The following day.

Scene Two: Late morning, the next day.

We have shared the incommunicable experience of war. We have felt, we still feel, the passion of life to its top ... In our youths our hearts were touched with fire.

Oliver Wendell Holmes

ACT ONE

Scene One

South Chicago, Illinois, 1956. A small quaint dining room. One exit leads to the kitchen, another exit leads to the rest of the house off-stage. A back door leads to the backyard which takes up the rest of the stage. The yard has a small flower garden, a bench, a small table and a few chairs, etc. A stairway leads to the upper balcony. A door leads to the basement.

On rise, a handsome, determined, powerful-looking young man enters into the backyard. This is SILVIO ROSATO. He is thirty-six years old and has an air of curiosity about him. He is dressed in a suit that is well-maintained and neat. He carries a suitcase. He looks around him. He crosses to the back door and knocks. He knocks again, but there is no answer. He sets his suitcase down, and walks about the yard. He makes his way to the stairway and begins to step up. He stops when he discovers that the wooden post to the stairway bannister is loose. He handles it a bit and then finds that the first step is loose as well. He begins to examine the problem as he removes the wooden post from its base. He handles it with authority.

Another man enters the yard from the lane. He too is dressed in a suit but not with the flair of SILVIO's. This is EDDIE, JR. He is thirty-two years old. He carries a briefcase. SILVIO turns to face him as he replaces the post back in its base. The two men look at each other. There is a quiet pause as the two take each other in. Finally EDDIE puts down his briefcase.

EDDIE
You must be my brother.

SILVIO
Eduardo?

EDDIE
Please, they call me Eddie here.

SILVIO
Eddie. (*shakes his hand*) Silvio. (*pause*) I'm sorry, I didn't mean to ...

EDDIE
I've been meaning to fix it.

SILVIO
The wood is rotted out at the base. I'll fix it for you.

EDDIE
This is quite a surprise. We didn't expect you till later.

SILVIO
I wasn't sure I was in the right place. I tried to enter the front, the door was locked.

EDDIE
This is America. You keep your doors locked, and your opinions to yourself. Especially here in Chicago.

SILVIO
I lived in Belgium for two years and nobody locked their doors. Same thing in Italy.

EDDIE
People here in America have the right to bear arms. If you just walked into a person's home, that person could interpret that as an invasion of their property. They would have the right to defend themselves. In a moment of panic, he could take his gun and shoot you. (*pause*) What did you do in Belgium?

SILVIO
Worked in the coal mines. Lived in a town called La Louvière.

EDDIE
Speak French?

SILVIO
Yes. So do my two girls. They come home from school, they speak Italian to Carmela, my wife, and then they recite a poem for me in French. It's just wonderful, you know, seeing your little girls have such ease with language. I'll show you some pictures ...

He checks the inside pocket of his jacket.

I'm sorry, how rude of me. How about you? How about your children?

EDDIE
I don't have any.

SILVIO
Oh. Well, there's time. I'm sure your wife will want children at some point.

EDDIE
I'm not married.

SILVIO
Oh. Well, there's time for that too.

There is an awkward pause.

EDDIE
Didn't Daddy tell you about us? The family here.

SILVIO
No. Last time I heard from your father ... Eduardo ... I received a suit from him. I was five years old. Actually the package was sent to my mother. That was the only real contact I ever had with him. I've been in Canada for two months, I decided I wanted to see him.

EDDIE
Yes. Well. There's been a question in my mind as to the purpose of your visit here. You called a month ago and my father hasn't been the same since. What did you say to him?

SILVIO
That I wanted to meet him. There's something I want to ask him.

13

EDDIE

You understand the concern I have for my parents?
They're getting old, and I don't need their lives disrupted.
Understand? You are the son he left behind. Lots of time has
passed. I don't know anything about you. I admit, I've been
very curious over the years. But we're not supposed to talk
about you. That was the law. And now you're here.

SILVIO

If you can direct me to Rita Testa's house, I'll be on my way. If
your father wants to see me, that's where I'll be.

EDDIE

What do you have in Canada? I mean, any friends, relatives?

SILVIO

No.

EDDIE

(*seems a little uneasy*) What are your plans?

SILVIO

In life? My plan is to set things right with my family.

EDDIE

Your family? You want to set things right ... you mean ...

SILVIO

Give them a life. My wife, my children. My mother. (*referring
to EDDIE's briefcase*) Are you going somewhere?

EDDIE

What, this? No, no. Actually I have an appointment ... it's
part of my job. My work is in there. I'm a salesman. I work
for an engraving company. Business cards, letterheads, that
sort of thing. My job is to travel the road, from company to
company and sell them our services. Every company needs a
business card, and a letterhead.

SILVIO

So you print information on a card?

EDDIE

Oh, no no no. This isn't printing. This is what you call engraving. Embossing. Let me show you.

Opens up his briefcase and takes out a few sample business cards and letterheads.

You see. Feel this. See how the print is raised? That's called embossing. It's classier than just a cheap old printed card. Feel this. Don't they have this in Italy?

SILVIO

I was never around any businessman.

EDDIE

Silvio. (*pause*) Why don't you come on in. Freshen up.

SILVIO

If it's okay with you I'd rather stay outside. The overnight train from Montreal is a long ride. I need some air, stretch my legs a bit. (*pause*) So where is Eduardo?

EDDIE

Pa is at work, he'll be here soon.

SILVIO

What does he do?

EDDIE

Works at an aluminum plant. He's a manager there. Runs the entire day shift.

SILVIO

And your mother?

EDDIE

She's probably at her social club. The Daughters of Columbus. It's a haven for old Italian women where they pick up gossip and rumours. It gives them a chance to brag about their children. It keeps her busy since she's had to retire. Arthritis.

SILVIO

So, Eduardo has done pretty well for himself.

EDDIE

Oh, yeah. Owns this house. Owns the one next to it. He rents that out. Ida lives upstairs here. My sister. My father has provided well for his family. I'm surprised you don't know all this.

SILVIO

Well like I said, there hasn't been much communication between Eduardo and I.

EDDIE

Eduardo? You're having a tough time calling him father.

SILVIO

I don't really know him as a father do I?

EDDIE

No. (*pause*) How old were you?

SILVIO

Eduardo left Italy when I was four months old. I was a baby. Growing up, they told me that my father went on a long trip and never came back.

The phone rings. EDDIE opens the back door and steps into the dining room.

EDDIE

(*on phone*) Hello. Yes he's here. We're having a chat. No, Ma. We're just talking. What? About things. Ma, I left a folder on the table, it's not here. Where?

He finds it on the seat of a chair.

Okay, I got it. No, I have an appointment. I'll wait for Ida. Fine. Good-bye. Ma, wait. (*pause*) Nothing. I'll see you later.

Re-enters the backyard.

My father came to Chicago in 1920, and you were four months old. So what happened during the war? I mean by 1939 you were a young man. What did you do?

SILVIO

I fought.

EDDIE

You fought in the war? I would've liked to have known that I had a brother who fought in the war.

SILVIO

I'm sure your father had reasons for keeping this away from you.

EDDIE

What earthly reason could that be?

SILVIO

Eddie, I have children of my own. Two little girls. Every day that I wake up all I think about is to protect them from the darkness of this world. And if you've seen what I saw, believe me, there is plenty of darkness out there.

EDDIE

My God, Silvio, how could you be so reasonable about this?

SILVIO

Is there any other choice? It's the past. Let it go. I did.

EDDIE

So you were in the army? Did you see any combat?

SILVIO

(*pause*) Let's not talk about that.

EDDIE

Silvio, please, let's skip the formalities here. If I'm to be your brother, I need to know what you went through. Sacrifices were asked of us. The President reminded us every day. They don't make men like Roosevelt anymore. It was a sad day when he passed away. But he drew the picture very clear for us. Somehow I got left out of the sacrificing. The army wouldn't take me due to my flat feet. And I've never felt good about that. So you can understand my wanting to know what my brother went through. (*pause*) So let's have it.

SILVIO

I was born June 4, 1920.

EDDIE

My father arrived in Chicago … October of 1920.

SILVIO

October 12, 1920. We were raised by my mother. My sister was four years old. Times were tough. Food was scarce, but we ate. I had the privilege of two years of schooling. Then I had to work. It was the only way to bring food to the table.

EDDIE

How old were you then?

SILVIO

Eight, nine years old. At that age, there wasn't much I could do. I hauled wood, worked on farms. We made it through. Then the war came along. I was drafted in 1940. I was sent to Egypt. My group was stationed at Fort Capuzzo. We were there for about a year and a half. We worked. We built roads. Mostly our work consisted of reclaiming the desert. Do you know what that means?

EDDIE

No.

SILVIO

Turning the sand back into fertile ground. It's very tedious work. But we did it.

EDDIE

Did you see battle?

SILVIO

Yes.

EDDIE

Did you fight the Americans?

SILVIO

No. This was 1941. So the Americans weren't there yet. I fought the British.

EDDIE

What happened?

SILVIO

I was eventually wounded, and captured by the British. I spent the remainder of the war as a prisoner of war. I was placed in a P.O.W. camp in England, a small town called Reading.

EDDIE

How did they treat you?

SILVIO

We Italians were fine. The Italian prisoners were allowed to work on farms, and estates, always under guard, but it removed us from the monotony of the camp.

EDDIE

So you met Germans?

SILVIO

I fought with them. In Africa, the Italian army was under direct control of the German command. That placed us, in effect, under the leadership of the Desert Fox. Erwin Rommel. I saw him.

EDDIE

You met the Desert Fox?

SILVIO

No. I saw him. From a distance of about ten metres. It was about a couple of weeks before the battle. And the German command had come to our base to lay down plans and instructions to our superior officers. It was during a food break. I remember getting up for more beans and bread, when my partner turned to me and said, "There he is. Rommel, the Desert Fox." I turned to look, and I expected this big tall man. Instead, I saw this very small simple man, sitting next to the soldiers eating the same food we were eating. If you blinked, you'd miss him. But there he was, a great commander with ordinary men. As I stood in line for more bread, I remember exchanging a glance with him. For that moment, that glance was frozen. His eyes were heavy with thought. I said to myself, The fate of all of our lives rest in your hands. The very decisions you make today will decide if I live or die. And his eyes said I know what you're thinking, but don't be afraid. And then he looked away and kept eating his beans and bread.

EDDIE

What was the battle like?

SILVIO

Eddie. I said as much as I'm going to say. Now let it go.

The phone rings. EDDIE opens the back door and steps into the dining room.

EDDIE

(*on phone*) Hello. No, Ma. We're just talking. Well there's no point in calling here every two minutes. I don't know ... the war ... why didn't you tell me he was in the war? Well ... why didn't Pa? I don't know, Ma, because he's my brother ... and I want to know these things. Ma ... I'm hanging up ... Ma. I'll see you later.

Hangs up. He gets a bottle of wine and pours two drinks. He gulps down one glass and pours himself another. He takes both glasses and steps out into the backyard. He hands SILVIO a glass. They clink glasses.

Salute.

SILVIO

Salute. (*drinks*) Does your father have any tools? I'll get to work on this post here. We can talk while I fix it.

EDDIE

(*unlocks the basement door with a key*) Okay. Just down to your left. There's tools and there should be some wood lying about. I never asked you what line of work you're in.

SILVIO

I'm a carpenter. Self-taught.

SILVIO exits. EDDIE gulps down his wine. He crosses to SILVIO's suitcase and examines it. He seems deep in thought. IDA enters the upper balcony. She is a thirty-five-year-old effervescent woman dressed with style and grace. She pins some clothes on the clothesline.

IDA

Eddie. Eddie! What are you, deaf? Don't forget to pick up Pa at work.

EDDIE

I can't. I have an appointment in half an hour.

IDA

Where?

EDDIE

Lakeshore Drive.

IDA

Well it's on the way. Just pick him up. Why are you drinking so early?

EDDIE

Will you shut up.

IDA

My God, Eddie, can you be more depressed? Lighten up, will you.

SILVIO re-enters the yard from the basement. He carries a hammer, saw and a piece of wood. He does not notice IDA. He sets down the tools and begins to remove his jacket.

Do not tell me, Lord in Heaven, that this is my brother.

She descends the stairs.

Are you my brother?

EDDIE

Silvio, this is Ida. Ida, Silvio. Our brother.

IDA

My God, you're a movie star. Welcome to America.

She dashes into his arms. SILVIO hugs her and then kisses her on both cheeks.

I'm Ida, and I'm very pleased to meet you. Why didn't you tell me he was here? So what ... Eddie's got you working already?

SILVIO

No, no, I just hate to see things broke like this. I said I would fix it.

EDDIE

Look, I'll get going, why don't you keep him company. Silvio, I'll be back in a couple of hours. Just make yourself comfortable. There's towels in the bathroom if you need to take a bath. And ... I'll see you later ...

IDA

Go already. Just don't be late for dinner.

EDDIE picks up his briefcase and exits through the house.

Don't mind Eddie, he's a little moosh. Hope he didn't bore you about his heartbreak. It's been four months now, he just can't get over that girl. So he drowns his sorrow in wine. Oh, look at me going on here ... so, when did you get here?

She makes her way into the dining room to pour herself a glass of wine. She continues talking.

Pa said you were arriving tonight? What difference is it anyway? You're here. Look at me rambling on. I'm just so excited to finally meet you. Here's to new family.

They clink glasses.

Cheers.

SILVIO

Salute.

IDA

You're so Italian. I love it. Let me fix you some lunch. You must be starving. I'll make you a sandwich.

SILVIO

I'm fine. I don't want to spoil my dinner.

IDA

You gotta have something. How about some fruit?

SILVIO

Now a piece of fruit I'll have. Do you have any grapes?

IDA

That's all my father eats. Where did you get those eyes?

SILVIO

That's from my mother's side. Her brother. I'm supposed to go visit his grave site.

IDA

He's buried in Chicago?

SILVIO

He lived here. He died in 1921.

IDA

Who are you talking about?

SILVIO

Pietro Colarelli.

IDA

Peter. Oh, my God. How stupid of me. You're talking about my mother's first husband. She can't even bring herself to visit his grave. Dying so young like that, I can't imagine it. Why do you want to go to his grave site?

SILVIO

I promised my mother I would lay down some flowers, and say a prayer.

IDA

That's so sweet. Come. Sit. Take a load off. (*pause*) You're a brave man, Silvio. Coming here to meet Daddy. That takes a lot of courage.

BOBBY

(*off-stage*) Ida!

BOBBY enters from the lane. He is thirty-seven years old and dressed in mechanic's cover-alls.

IDA

Silvio, this is my husband Robert.

BOBBY

Well well well. Look at this. Good to meet you, Silvio. (*shakes his hand*) You can call me Bobby.

He kisses IDA.

How'ya doin' honey? Old man Turdy had to go to the hospital. Trouble breathing. So we closed up the shop.

IDA

Bobby is a mechanic.

BOBBY

What's wrong with Junior?

IDA

Don't call him that, you know it bothers him.

BOBBY

I tell ya, Silvio, we gotta get you a nice hot rod so you can start cruising the chicks with your brother. He needs a woman to make him whole again.

IDA

Four years my brother was with his girl, close to getting married. All the travelling Eddie does. A girl wants some stability in her life, and Eddie just wasn't giving it to her.

BOBBY

That's not all he wasn't giving her. How the hell can a man do the deed, if he's two hundred miles clear across the state? You know what I'm talking about, Silvio. I told Junior a hundred times, before you go off on one of your business trips, make sure you pay a visit to your girl. Get an oil change. Lube job. The whole works. It's gotta be that way, or the girl just loses her desire for you.

IDA

You're so crass. Eddie was doing right by that girl, she just didn't appreciate him.

BOBBY

Oh, Ida, stop treating him like a baby. What do you think, Silvio?

SILVIO

I think if there is true love between a man and a woman, they would wait for each other. He for her, and she for him.

BOBBY

Well this is America, buddy. And people don't like waiting over here. It's all rush rush rush. You gotta grab it, while the grabbing is good. Well, what's done is done. I ain't gonna argue with you. Ida, I went to the plant to pick up your daddy, and he wasn't there.

IDA

I just sent Eddie to go pick him up.

BOBBY

Why did you do that? I told you I was going to do it.

IDA

You said you couldn't.

BOBBY

I said I couldn't pick up your mother. Man, doesn't anybody listen around here. People in this family have to start registering the information that is spoken to them. That's what hearing and memory is for. I'm telling you, Silvio, married into this family means you do a lot of repeat conversation. Been doing it for ten years. Nobody gets it the first time, so you may as well say it again.

IDA

Okay, let's not make a big to-do about it.

BOBBY

(*pause*) You're gonna like Chicago. I'll show you around. Great city. Got two baseball teams. The Cubs and the White Sox. Me, I'm White Sox all the way. You into baseball? (*pause*) You know ... the old pastime, America's game. (*pause*) I guess it's nothing but soccer out there, isn't it?

SILVIO

(*opens his suitcase*) I have something for you.

He removes a suit for a five-year-old boy from 1925.

Do you have children? Eduardo sent me this when I was five years old. It's still good ... it would be a shame to throw it away.

IDA

We don't have children. Bobby and I wanted to wait till we got comfortable with ...

BOBBY

(*leans on the bannister*) Comfortable with what, Ida? Children just get in the way when you're trying to build a life. Don't ask for something you don't want, that's my motto.

The post gives way and causes BOBBY to fall down.

God damn it! What is wrong with Eddie! Doesn't he ever fix anything around here? He can't expect your father to do everything. Look at that, nearly tore my shirt. Just pisses me off. Maybe you can start to set things right around here. You look like a man they'll listen to. God knows they don't listen to me.

IDA

(*takes the suit*) Thank you. That's very kind of you.

SILVIO

(*removes a piece of provolone cheese from his suitcase*) This is for all of you. Homemade provolone. (*removes a bottle from his suitcase*) This here is olive oil.

IDA

Homemade?

SILVIO

Oh, yes. We make everything back home.

He removes a beautiful hand-woven tablecloth.

This is for your table.

IDA

Oh my God. Feel this.

BOBBY
    What is it?

IDA
    It's a tablecloth, silly. Feels like I'm holding a baby. So soft.
    Thank you, Silvio. This is so nice of you.

    *IDA crosses into the house. She places the suit and the bottle on the
    table and exits.*

BOBBY
    So what are your plans? You lookin' to live here?

SILVIO
    No. It's just a visit.

BOBBY
    Going back to Italy?

SILVIO
    Canada.

BOBBY
    Canada? Isn't that far?

SILVIO
    It's just across the border. Montreal.

BOBBY
    Montreal? I thought that was in Paris.

SILVIO
    Paris is in France. Montreal is in Canada.

BOBBY
    Well. I'm not one for geography. So where d'ya learn to speak
    English so well?

SILVIO
    In prison.

BOBBY
    Did some time, huh?

SILVIO

Time?

BOBBY

Served time. What were you in for?

SILVIO

I was a prisoner of war.

BOBBY

Holy shit! You were a P.O.W.? Man I heard about them prison camps. The torture. The mind games. Brutal stuff, man. How did the Germans treat you?

SILVIO

I was a prisoner of the British.

BOBBY

You fought the British?

SILVIO

In Egypt.

BOBBY

Egypt?

IDA re-enters the yard with some grapes for SILVIO.

Ida, did you know that Silvio was in the war?

SILVIO

(*to IDA*) Thank you.

BOBBY

You saw the pyramids?

SILVIO

Yes.

IDA

The pyramids ... that must've been so romantic.

BOBBY

What the hell is so romantic about a pyramid? It's a friggin' three-sided triangle.

SILVIO
Oh, it's more than that. It's the mystery of a civilization. The pyramids represent everything that's great about mankind.

BOBBY
You think so?

SILVIO
How old is this house?

BOBBY
I'd give it forty, fifty years.

SILVIO
Let's even say a hundred. It's falling apart. The pyramids have stood for over four thousand years. No repairs needed.

BOBBY
Well they built things to last back then, I'll give you that. I just don't see how they're romantic, that's all.

IDA
Oh, Bobby, you're all cars and carburetors.

BOBBY
Did you fight Americans?

SILVIO
No. I fought the English.

BOBBY
But you were on the same side that was against the Americans.

IDA
Bobby ... he's tired ... can we talk later ...

BOBBY
It's just conversation. What's the big deal? We're getting to know each other. Isn't that right? (*pause*) If you fought for Italy, that means you fought for Mussolini. That means you fought for the Fascists. Were you a Fascist?

SILVIO
No.

BOBBY

But you fought for the Fascists?

SILVIO

I was not part of the Fascist Army. I was a soldier in the King's Army. There were two sections within Italy's military. You had the Fascists, and then you had the King's Army.

BOBBY

Italy had a king?

SILVIO

Vittorio Emmanuele the Third. He was our king. Mussolini was in charge of the government.

BOBBY

And you fought for the king. You sure did. I was drafted you know. Did my basic training at Fort Sam Houston, Alabama. Man ... my unit ... we were ready to take on those Germans. Fucking Krauts. But before we got called up, the war was over, and that was that.

The phone rings. IDA re-enters the house.

IDA

Bobby!

BOBBY enters the house. She grabs the phone.

Hello. No, Ma, he's here. I sent Eddie to get Daddy. How was I supposed to know? Okay, I'll send him. Bye.

Hangs up the phone. The phone rings.

Hello. What do you mean? Where could he be? Okay. We'll wait here. G'bye. (*hangs up the phone*)

BOBBY

(*picks up the suit from the table*) What's he trying to do, rub it in my face? Doesn't he know we can't have children?

IDA

Forget that. Eddie just called. You have to go pick up my mom. Eddie went to the plant to get my dad. He never showed up for work.

BOBBY

Well I'll be damned. He hasn't missed a day's work in thirty years.

IDA

Where could he be?

BOBBY

Ida, your father is meeting his son for the first time since he was born.

IDA

Look at him out there. He has no idea what his presence here is doing to my father.

BOBBY

Hey listen, baby. If you ask me, it's a good thing that two grown men get their shit in order, you know what I mean. One's the father, one's the son. They've lived without each other from the beginning. A little bit of reconciling will do them both some good. Now you mind the fort, get to know him. He's as scared as your father, trust me.

IDA

Why would they be scared?

BOBBY

One is scared for not knowing the other. One is scared for not wanting to know the other. Which is which is what they're gonna have to work out.

He kisses her and exits.
IDA makes her way back into the yard. She stares at SILVIO. He smiles.

SILVIO

I'll get started on this.

The lights fade to black.

Scene Two

In black we hear the sound of a handsaw sawing wood, and nails being hammered. On rise, we see SILVIO hammering away at the last nail on the first step of the stairway. He's removed his jacket, shirt and tie and they rest neatly on his suitcase. He's dressed in an undershirt. As he completes his work, RITA, a young girl twenty-two years of age, steps into the yard from the lane holding a book. She is a sweet, shy, attractive young girl. She watches SILVIO with a degree of awe.

SILVIO has hammered in his last nail. He gets up and pounds his foot on the first step. The step is secure. With some force, he now tries to shake the post. It doesn't move. It's sturdy and solid. Content with his work, he steps back and admires it. A smile forms on his face. He turns and now notices RITA.

SILVIO
Rita?

He grabs her and swings her in his arms.

Rita, come stai?

RITA
Bene, grazie. E voi?

SILVIO
(*kisses her on both cheeks*) Benissimo! Ti sei fatta una giovinetta!

RITA
Grazie. E tu, hai fatto un ... come se dice ... un buon viaggio?
Mi devi scusare, l'italiano non l'ho parli troppo bene.

SILVIO
Invece tu lo parli abastanza bene. We could speak English if
you like? My God, Rita. I remember when you were a baby,
I'd hold you in my arms, I'd feed you some fruit, you'd burp
all over me because I kept tickling you and throwing you up
in the air. Your mother kept telling me, "Easy with the baby,
she'll throw up all over you." And you know what, Rita, I didn't
mind. How's your mother and father?

RITA

They're fine. They're waiting for you.

SILVIO

I miss them so much. They're so kind and gentle. Look at you. You have no idea the joy you brought into my life when you were born. I was fourteen years old. I never really knew happiness in my life till that day. When I first laid eyes upon you, I just wanted to smother you with all my heart. I knew then that I wanted children of my own. (*pause*) It was a sad day when your family left for America.

RITA

We're together now. How's Carmela?

SILVIO

(*puts his shirt and tie back on*) She's fine. She's in Italy with the children. Do you come here often?

RITA

No. Our families are not close.

SILVIO

Why is that? (*pause*) Rita, you can talk to me.

RITA

Your father is a very difficult man. He stays away from people.

SILVIO

Do you get along with Eddie and Ida?

RITA

Ida takes me for a soda once in a while, we listen to the latest records. We go shopping. I don't see Eddie much. School keeps me busy.

SILVIO

They don't seem to know much about me. Why is that?

RITA

Your father forbids his family to speak of his past. Ida tells me. Now that you're here, well, his past has caught up with him. He and my father had an argument just the other day.

SILVIO

Over what? (*pause*) Rita.

RITA

When we got your telegram that said you were coming, my
father came over here to talk and ... you know ... that what a
good thing it was that you were coming ... and then one
thing led to another ... it was ugly.

SILVIO

He said he was glad to finally meet me.

RITA

Your father hasn't seen you since you were a little baby. And
based on what I know of that man, he does not regret one
single action from his past. (*pause*) What's wrong?

SILVIO

It's nothing.

RITA

Is it your war wound? (*pause*) I kept all your letters that you
sent my parents from Egypt.

SILVIO

I thought about you so much when I was there.

RITA

We were so scared for you. We didn't know day to day if we
were ever going to hear from you again. I'm glad those days
are over.

SILVIO

I was never going to die. Not there. I refused to die in a desert
away from those I love. I willed it to happen. Two things kept
me alive. Music. At the base, my commanding officer had these
records. Verdi, Puccini, Rossini, I learnt everything there was to
know about opera. Its beauty, its majesty and its healing
powers. Do you like music?

RITA

Yes. What was the second thing? (*pause*) You said two things
kept you alive. Music was one, what was the second thing?

SILVIO

I'll tell you another time.

RITA

Why did you stop writing? My parents used to read your letters to me. I thought you lost interest in me.

SILVIO

I would never do that. Never.

RITA

Then what happened? Tell me.

SILVIO

You want me to talk of war to a little girl.

RITA

I'm a woman, Silvio. I'm strong.

SILVIO

In school, did they teach you about Halfaya Pass?

RITA

No.

SILVIO

(*silent for a second as he takes it all back in*) My battalion was sent to Halfaya Pass.

RITA

Where is that?

SILVIO

It's a stretch of land about two hundred kilometres in northern Africa that goes into Libya. I was sent to the front there. Close to the border on the Egyptian side. This was the battle for Halfaya Pass. We were placed on a desert hill. We were waiting for a British convoy. It was to be an ambush. Instead, a small scouting party walked into our trap. No real danger to us. I told my sergeant, "Fire warning shots. We can take them prisoner." But no! We had orders from the German command. I begged the sergeant, "Do the right thing, or God will punish us!" He screamed, "Open fire!"

RITA

Did you?

SILVIO

It was a turkey shoot. The entire Italian platoon opened fire.
And we just kept firing. And firing. Again. And again. We
slaughtered an entire scouting party that could've easily been
taken prisoner. Our guns mowed them down with no mercy.
The British sent in reinforcements and surrounded us. And
the real battle began. We were overrun by the superior British
forces. I ran out of ammunition and ran for cover. A grenade
exploded maybe twenty metres from me where I saw my
partner torn to pieces. Shrapnel ripped right through my leg.
The burning pain was unbearable.

RITA

My God …

SILVIO

I refused to die. I waited for the cover of night. I ripped off
my pant leg and made a tourniquet to stop the bleeding. It
took me two days to crawl on my stomach with one good leg
but I made it back to base. I lived off of my own blood. I had
no water. Nothing but my own blood. When I got to base …
it had been destroyed. I knew if I waited there, I would
eventually meet up with the enemy, but I passed out. When I
came to, a rifle was aimed right at me. I locked eyes with my
British foe, I could see his name on his uniform. Wilson. Our
eyes met, and for a moment I thought I was a dead man. The
pain was so unbearable, I wanted the soldier to relieve me of
my pain by shooting me. Then I thought no. I cannot die. I
will not die. For a moment it looked like the end, but Wilson
disarmed, and called for the medics. They quickly bandaged
my leg. A little unexpected kindness can go a long way in life.

RITA

What did they do?

SILVIO

The British … they could not take any prisoners, because they
were still under heavy fire. I was to be on my own. I waited

and waited ... I heard the heavy fire of artillery. The battle for Halfaya Pass raged on. The British later came to call it Hellfire Pass. And if it wasn't hell that night, then hell truly does not exist. Finally the British had succeeded in fortifying their positions, and had taken the entire unit prisoner ... the survivors. I was placed on a ship, encircled the entire African continent, and brought to England where I spent the remainder of the war as a P.O.W. (*pause*) When I go to sleep at night, I can still see their faces. The blood. I hear the sounds. The sounds ... I killed men, Rita. I became a killer out in that desert.

RITA
(*crying*) Sshhh. Don't say that. My God ...

SILVIO
I stopped writing because I wanted to protect you from myself. I wanted to protect those I love by keeping them away from me.

RITA
Please, don't say that.

SILVIO
That's what I thought until I met Carmela. And she gave me hope, and my life back.

RITA
I don't want you to be hurt anymore. I don't want that hope destroyed here on this visit.

SILVIO
Rita. Nothing can destroy me. I looked death right in the face in that desert. And I frightened it away. I cannot die. I will not be destroyed. And nothing scares me. Let's not speak of the past anymore. Rita, do you still remember the poem I taught you? Recite it for me.

RITA
My Italian is not as good anymore ...

SILVIO
Do it for me, Rita. I know you can. Go ahead ...

RITA is about to recite the poem.

Ah, ah ... wait.

He takes a seat on the bench. She's about to begin again.

Ah, no ...

RITA
Right.

She curtseys.

San Pasquale Bailone
Protettore delle donne
Fam'aver un bel marito
Bianco, rosso e colorito
Come te, tale quale
O glorioso San Pasquale

SILVIO
(*applauds*) Brava! Bravissima! You were three years old when I taught you that poem. You recite that once a day, and you will be protected. A man will eventually come your way and make you his princess.

IDA enters from the upper house.

IDA
Rita. What a surprise. Isn't my brother gorgeous?

SILVIO
I'll put these tools away.

He collects the tools and exits into the basement.

RITA
Why isn't your father here to greet him? It's the least he could do.

IDA
We weren't sure what time he was coming.

RITA
Didn't anyone think to call the train station?

IDA

You're jumpy today. Was Silvio insulted? Did he tell you
something? Have you been crying?

RITA

No. I have to go to the library.

IDA

Rita, baby, what did he say? Did he say something to hurt
you?

RITA

He would never hurt me. Never.

IDA

Why don't you stay for dinner? We'll all spend the evening
together.

RITA

He's staying with us.

SILVIO re-enters the yard from the basement.

SILVIO

Ida, why don't I come back later. I've kept Rita's parents
waiting.

IDA

You're not staying here? In your father's house?

SILVIO

I wasn't invited. May I go wash my hands?

IDA

Yes you may.

SILVIO steps into the house and exits.

My father hasn't been himself for a month now.

RITA

You and Eddie are going to have to find a way to control
your father. He's unpredictable. I really have to get to the
library.

IDA

Rita, wait. Will you stay a while? I want you here. There's no telling what those two are going to say to each other. You know the way my dad gets. Rita, please.

RITA

I'd have to ask my parents.

IDA

I'll come with you. We'll go to the library first.

BOBBY

(*off-stage*) Ida! Ida, we're back!

IDA

(*to RITA*) Hold on. Let me check on my mother ...

She makes her way to the back door.

SILVIO enters the dining room with a glass of water and begins to make his way out back, as BOBBY enters with a box of groceries. ANGELINA follows behind him. She is a fifty-eight-year-old woman and walks with a cane. SILVIO turns around to face her. They stare at each other for a moment.

BOBBY

Ma, this is Silvio. Silvio, this is your ... er ... this is Angelina.

ANGELINA

(*takes a good look at SILVIO's face*) C'ai l'occhi di tùo zio.

SILVIO

(*kissing her on both cheeks*) Piacere.

BOBBY

Well, if you guys are gonna be talking Italian, I won't understand anything.

ANGELINA

I said he has his uncle's eyes. You have to excuse these American boys, Silvio, they never learnt to speak Italian.

BOBBY

It's America, Ma. We speak American here.

ANGELINA
It doesn't matter, you could still have learnt the language of
your parents.

BOBBY
The language of the Tardelli family is American. Nothing I
could do about that.

IDA
Ma, I'll be back in a minute ...

*ANGELINA steps out into the backyard. SILVIO and BOBBY follow
her out.*

ANGELINA
Ida, wait, I forgot the pastries. Get a dozen cannoli ... Is that
Rita out there? You cute little thing. Are you dating anybody?

IDA
Ma!

ANGELINA
I can't ask a simple question? You're old enough to marry,
you know?

RITA
The right man hasn't found me yet.

*BOBBY begins to ascend the stairs. He stops to inspect the newly
fixed bannister. He seems impressed.*

BOBBY
You tell her, Rita. No point in rushing into something you'll
regret later.

IDA
Ma, we're going to the library, we'll be right back.

She exits with RITA.

ANGELINA
Don't forget the cannoli! Always running off, these kids.
Nobody has the time to get married anymore. Back in the
day, we settled first, then we decided what we wanted to do.

41

It's all reverse now. People have to go find themselves before they settle in.

BOBBY

People have to know each other before they get married, Ma.

ANGELINA

What do you know, you're half an idiot.

BOBBY

I get no respect in this house. None. You watch your way around here, Silvio. They'll be insulting you in no time.

ANGELINA

Ma va'fanculo!

BOBBY

You call me idiot every day. Silvio, do I look like an idiot to you? (*pause*) I'll be upstairs if you need anything. I want to check in on Turdy.

ANGELINA

What's wrong with Turdy?

BOBBY

Had trouble breathing this morning.

ANGELINA

Oh my. Hope it's not serious.

BOBBY

He'd be fine if he didn't have to breathe. Catch you guys later.

He ascends the stairs and exits.

ANGELINA

He's a good boy. He's just a little slow in the head. That's what happens when you listen to all that loud music they play these days. They call it rock 'n' roll. Silvio, dear, if you go in the kitchen, you'll find a watering can by the sink. Fill it up with water, will you?

SILVIO exits into the kitchen.

Your father should be home soon. (*pause*) So you met your
brother?

SILVIO

(*off-stage*) Yes.

ANGELINA

He's a good man. I wish he were married though. You're
married, aren't you?

SILVIO

I was twenty-eight when I got married.

He re-enters with a watering can.

ANGELINA

Who did you marry at twenty-eight?

SILVIO

Carmela Ialongo. The daughter of Domenico and Clelia
Ialongo. She wasn't born yet when you left Italy. She's ten
years younger than me.

ANGELINA

Ten years? Maybe you can tell your brother there's hope for
him yet.

She takes the watering can.

SILVIO

Let me get that for you.

ANGELINA

No, no, the doctor says I need the exercise. Gotta find a way
to keep these bones moving. Otherwise they dry up. Besides,
who else is gonna water these plants? (*pause*) I guess you'll be
wanting to visit your uncle's grave? I know your mother would
want that. How is Filomena?

SILVIO

She's as good as a mother can be.

43

ANGELINA

> Tuberculosis. (*pause*) That's what he died of, your uncle. It was awful. He never had a chance. We never had a chance. He was already in Chicago when you were born. A brave man, Peter was. Coming here all by himself, to start a new life, a better life. Came back to Italy to pick me up. Your father. And Rita's parents. Your father paid for their trip. We were to build a life here. All of us. Then Peter got sick on the ship. He had the whole future in front of him. And then it's just snatched away like that. Everything just started to fall apart after that. Rita's parents went back to Italy. I was all alone. Just wasn't fair.

SILVIO

> I'm sorry.

ANGELINA

> Oh, don't be sorry. Nothing could be done. It was a mystery disease. The doctors themselves were helpless. (*pause*) Well, Silvio, you may as well ask and get it off your chest. Especially now that your father's not here.

SILVIO

> Ask what?

ANGELINA

> What happened thirty-six years ago.

SILVIO

> That's not on my mind at all.

ANGELINA

> You're not even curious?

SILVIO

> What good will that information do me? What happened, happened. That was the past. No use living out the past.

ANGELINA

> Certainly your mother discussed this with you.

SILVIO

> She told me things.

ANGELINA

Well there you go. She told you things. I was married to her
brother, and he died. Then I married your father. You
must've formed an opinion of your father and me?

SILVIO

Angelina. If it's okay with you, I wish not to discuss my mother.

ANGELINA

Your father is going to bring it up.

SILVIO

Then let him bring it up. I'm not here to discuss the actions
of his past.

ANGELINA

So you're okay with everything that happened?

SILVIO

I really don't know what happened, do I?

ANGELINA

(*pause*) He saved me, your father. When your uncle Peter died,
I was ready to throw myself into the lake. And I was desperate
enough to do it. When we arrived here, your father was living
with us. But your uncle got sick on the ship. Peter got sick,
and your father did everything he could to make him
comfortable. We knew he was dying. And I just couldn't cope.

SILVIO

Angelina. I really don't want to hear this.

ANGELINA

Well you may as well hear it, young man, because your father
hasn't been able to sleep for a month. You called a month
ago saying you were going to pay a visit, and he hasn't been
able to shut his eyes since. Certainly you expect some of this
to come out?

SILVIO

I expect nothing. That's not why I'm here.

ANGELINA

Then why are you here? (*pause*) Your mother never intended to come to Chicago. She left him to dry all alone here. Your father couldn't go back to get her, because she made it clear that she was not coming over. He wanted his children here.

SILVIO

He wanted me here?

ANGELINA

And your sister. He couldn't go back. She made it clear. That's what happened.

SILVIO

If that's what happened, then that's what happened. Let the past live with the past.

ANGELINA

Your mother was a very difficult woman back in the day. She always had to have her way. She was difficult to please.

SILVIO

(*emphatically*) Let's not talk about my mother!

ANGELINA

It's fine. I just wanted you to know our side of the story. We won't speak of it anymore.

She's finished watering the flowers.

It's good to finally meet you.

ANGELINA enters the house, as EDDIE enters the dining room. He drops his briefcase on the table. Grabs the bottle of wine and two glasses.

What took you so long?

EDDIE

Made a great sale! Yes I did. Sold them a hundred thousand business cards, and two hundred thousand letterheads. That's a pretty tall order for a medium-sized company.

ANGELINA

Good for you, sonny. Where's your father? Didn't you go pick him up?

EDDIE

I went, Ma. He never showed up for work.

ANGELINA

Oh, dear. I hope nothing happened. Should we call the hospitals?

EDDIE

Nothing happened, Ma. He took the day off is all.

ANGELINA

He never takes a day off.

EDDIE

Well this day he did. Nothing wrong in that. A man works thirty years for the same company, he's entitled to a day off.

He enters into the backyard. ANGELINA follows him.

ANGELINA

Rita was here to see you. Why don't you marry that girl? She's so adorable. She's looking for someone to find her.

EDDIE

She's too young for me, Ma.

ANGELINA

Silvio's wife is ten years younger than him.

EDDIE

Really?

SILVIO

Ten years and two days.

EDDIE

I'm not having this discussion with you.

He pours himself and SILVIO each a glass of wine.

ANGELINA

(*to SILVIO*) Talk some sense into him. I need to rest and take
my medicine. (*pause*) Your father is searching for the right
things to say to you.

She exits into the house.

EDDIE

Can you believe my mother?

SILVIO

A parent always wishes to see their children settled.

EDDIE

I'm settled, Silvio. I'm settled. I just don't like being treated
like a child.

They clink glasses.

Salute. It's not like I don't think of getting married. It's just
not in the cards right now.

He notices the bannister.

Look at that. Brand new. You're fast. I appreciate it. Now
maybe Daddy won't bother me anymore about fixing it. Let me
get another one. Another glass won't hurt.

*EDDIE steps into the dining room. SILVIO takes a seat at the patio
table and shuts his eyes to rest. EDDIE gets another bottle of wine,
when EDUARDO steps in. EDUARDO is a sixty-year-old man. He
has an air of impatience about him. Thirty-six years of unspoken
feelings have ravaged his looks.*

EDDIE

Pa. Where the hell were you?

*EDUARDO looks EDDIE in the face and says nothing. He pushes
EDDIE aside and watches SILVIO through the back door window.
EDUARDO steps slowly into the yard. EDDIE stays behind in the
dining room watching; he pours himself a glass of wine and drinks.
SILVIO senses a presence, he opens his eyes and rises. The two men
look at each other, each one waiting for the other to make the first
move. Finally, EDUARDO moves forward with his hand out.*

EDUARDO
Silvio.

SILVIO slowly gives him his hand and they shake.

Figlio mio.

SILVIO
Eduardo.

SILVIO's salutation seems to stab EDUARDO in the heart. EDUARDO scans every inch of SILVIO's body, takes SILVIO's hand and examines it.

EDUARDO
I remember that birth mark right there.

EDUARDO kisses SILVIO's hand.

I'll never forget it. (*pause*) You look good. Come stai? Stai bene? It's good to see you. I wasn't sure what time you were coming. (*pause*) How's your mother? (*pause*) Silvio ... Silvio ...

He embraces SILVIO and kisses him on both cheeks.

Anything you need, you just ask. Understand? Anything. I'm your father. Allow me to be your father now. You have family here. It's important that you believe this. My God! Your eyes. You have your uncle's eyes. That look. I can't explain it. Just like your uncle Peter's. I never thought I'd see those eyes again. (*pause*) How long are you staying?

SILVIO
Not long.

EDUARDO
You're not going to give me time to—to get to know you?

SILVIO
Is that what you want?

EDUARDO
Yes. I want to know everything about you. You're my first-born son.

EDDIE finally makes his way into the backyard. He hands the two men glasses of wine. They all clink glasses and drink.

EDUARDO

Salute. A la famiglia. Where is everyone?

EDDIE

Ma is taking a nap.

EDUARDO

Why? Is she sick?

EDDIE

You know she likes to nap before dinner.

EDUARDO

Nap? She doesn't do anything all day. Where's your sister?

EDDIE

I don't know.

EDUARDO

And Bobby?

SILVIO

Bobby is upstairs.

EDUARDO

Where's Ida?

EDDIE

I just told you, I don't know.

SILVIO

She's with Rita.

EDUARDO

Rita? What does that girl want? Why can't everybody be here? I made it clear I wanted everyone here when Silvio arrives! You have to excuse this family. They develop American ways here real fast. They forget their roots. Nothing matters to them. I'm telling you, this country welcomes the immigrants, but then they expect you to spit out all your culture.

EDDIE
That's not true.

EDUARDO
Then why don't you speak Italian? It's a simple question. If
you think we Italians have kept our culture here, then it
begins with knowing the language. Where's your language?
Silvio, that's one thing you can start doing with your brother
and sister, teach them Italian. God knows I've tried.

EDDIE
No you haven't.

EDUARDO
You saying I didn't try to teach you Italian at the table?

EDDIE
You made sure I spoke English, you wanted me to find my
place in this country.

EDUARDO
You have flat feet. You don't know what you're talking about.

*IDA enters the yard carrying a box of cannoli, RITA follows
carrying a bowl covered with a dish cloth.*

Where have you been? A man comes home from work, he
wants to eat.

IDA
Rita is having dinner with us tomorrow.

EDUARDO
Doesn't your mother cook?

IDA
What kind of way is that to talk?

EDUARDO
She knows I'm joking. Rita, you know I'm joking. I like this
girl. You're welcome for dinner, you know that. You remember
my son here?

RITA

Of course. He's like a brother to me. My mother made these.
(*to SILVIO*) Your favourite. Wine biscuits. Just for you.

EDUARDO

But we have pastries. What do we need more biscuits for?

RITA

I can take them back.

EDUARDO

You're gonna take them back now, and make me look like a
fool?

RITA

My mother didn't know you had pastries, I can take them back.

EDUARDO

You're not taking them back, don't be stupid, Rita.

SILVIO

Don't call her stupid.

> *EDUARDO withdraws towards the gate. IDA and RITA exit into
> the house.*

EDUARDO

(*turning around*) It's good to see my two boys together for the
first time. (*notices the bannister*) You fixed this?

EDDIE

No. Silvio did.

EDUARDO

This is your work? Who taught you how to do this?

EDDIE

Self-taught, Pa.

EDUARDO

Self-taught? I've been telling this chooch here from when he
was born. Learn something that will last a lifetime.

EDDIE

I have a job.

EDUARDO

You're a salesman. You call that a job? I'm talking about a trade, a craft, something you can touch. Something that will last.

EDDIE

Pa, this whole country is based on selling something. You think the President doesn't sell us? He does it every day.

EDUARDO

You watch what you say about Eisenhower. That is a great man, a great leader. And he's a hero. How can you reduce the President of the United States to a simple salesman?

EDDIE

I'm not. He's more than that. But selling is a natural part of leading.

EDUARDO

Please, Eddie. Your flat feet have made your brain moosh.

EDDIE

Why am I having this discussion?

EDUARDO

You brought it up.

EDDIE

I brought it up? Okay, you know what, Pa. I'm going inside to freshen up.

He exits.

EDUARDO

He's got a short fuse, that one. He never listens, he does what he wants.

SILVIO

He makes an honest living.

EDUARDO

It's a living. I don't know if it's useful. This is really good work. You can make a lot of money here in Chicago with a talent like this. How was your trip?

SILVIO
I read most of the way.

EDUARDO
You like to read?

SILVIO
Yes. Mostly history. I love geography too. I can study maps all day.

EDUARDO
How's your life? Are you happy?

SILVIO
I have a wonderful wife. I married Carmela Ialongo.

EDUARDO
Is she good to you?

SILVIO
I don't know what I'd do without her. I have two daughters. I brought some pictures if you want to see them.

He removes a few photographs from his jacket.

This is Maria. My first-born. Six years old. She's strong-willed and independent. She knows what she wants and goes after it. This here is Liliana. She's four years old. She has a smile all day. The most peaceful thing I've ever known. She never argues. And she's always by my side.

EDUARDO
Beautiful. Wonderful. You didn't waste any time did you? You got right to it.

SILVIO
And it's not over. She's pregnant.

EDUARDO
When? I mean ... when do you expect ... ?

SILVIO
Any day now. This one's going to be a boy. I just know it.

EDUARDO
Why is that?

SILVIO
Every man wishes to have a boy at some point. The boy
carries the name. That's very important to me.

EDUARDO
You want to be remembered? They forget you. That's the way
of this generation.

SILVIO
Not with me. I'm going to do right by this boy. And he will be
proud of the name. The Rosato name.

EDUARDO
Every man wishes to do right for his boy. It doesn't always
work out that way. Life happens too fast. You run out of time.

SILVIO
Life is long. There is always time to do right.

EDUARDO
(*pause*) You have a beautiful family, Silvio. I wish I was there.
How's your sister? How does her husband treat her? The word
I got from Italy is that he beats her. Tell me, I want to know.

SILVIO
I tried to stop him from beating her, but I was a boy, and I
just didn't have the strength to take him on.

EDUARDO
Did he beat you?

SILVIO
A few times. I'd rather he hit me than my sister.

EDUARDO
That bastard.

SILVIO
When I got back from the war, it was a different story. It was
the day before I was to be married. I heard some screaming
in the house.

EDUARDO

    Whose house?

SILVIO

    Mine ... yours. The house I lived in. My mother called out for help. I ran immediately to her. She had been hit ... I sat her down ... and I went into the house. He was beating my sister. He warned me to get out of the house ... that it wasn't my business. I told him to stop beating my sister. He came at me ... he had a piece of wood in his hands. I disarmed him, and gave him the beating of his life. For all the times he hit me as a boy, for all the times he beat my sister and for the one time he hit my mother. I sent him to the hospital. He laid charges. I had to pay a fine. The next day at my wedding, he refused to let his children come and celebrate with us.

EDUARDO

    What happened after?

SILVIO

    He never touched her again. I make my point just once.

EDUARDO

    Do you talk to him?

SILVIO

    No point in holding grudges.

EDUARDO

    You'd tell me if there was anything more?

SILVIO

    Even if there was, what could you do about it? You're here, and she's in Italy.

EDUARDO

    (*hands SILVIO back the photographs*) You stay close to them.

SILVIO

    Always.

EDUARDO

    What do they say about me? Back in the village?

SILVIO
That's the past. I'm not here to discuss the past.

EDUARDO
You can give an old man the satisfaction of knowing what he left back in his homeland.

SILVIO
You should go back and see for yourself.

EDUARDO
I can't go back. My life is here.

SILVIO
For a visit.

EDUARDO
That will never happen.

SILVIO
Why not?

EDUARDO
I don't think I'd be welcomed. Not after what I did.

SILVIO
(*pause*) Yes. Well. What you did ...

EDUARDO
When I left. (*pause*) Do you think about it?

SILVIO
No. Never.

EDUARDO
I don't believe you. You never in your life thought once about what happened?

SILVIO
I thought about it once.

EDUARDO
Once? You're lying.

SILVIO

I never tell a lie.

EDUARDO

That isn't human. Come on, let's just drop all this nonsense.
You're telling me right now ... standing in front of your
father for the first time, that you've never been curious? How
can that be?

SILVIO

Because if I allowed myself to be curious, it would mean that
at some point I'd have to feel sorry for myself. And my mother.
Feeling sorry gets you nowhere in life. I just accepted what
was given me, and moved on. That's how I survived.

EDUARDO

I see it in your eyes. You may think that in your head, but I
see it in your eyes.

SILVIO

You can see what you want to see. I'm not here for an
explanation.

EDUARDO

Well you're gonna get one, son. You're gonna get one, because
that's the only way I can move forward here. You need to know
that it wasn't all my fault. She's as much to blame as I am.

SILVIO

Who?

EDUARDO

Your mother. I came here with the good intention of starting
a new life. I didn't want to live like a poor man. In America
there was opportunity and a chance to start fresh. Your uncle
Peter was right. He told his sister, *your mother*, that the future
was here in America. Your mother was a stubborn mule. She
thought we could make a life there in Italy. But there was no
work, no hope. After you were born, it put even more
pressure on me to make a living. I had two children to feed.
So I came to Chicago with your uncle. Your mother begged

me not to come. I told her it might take a year for me to settle in, and then I would send her money to bring her over with you and your sister. But during that year ... Uncle Peter got sick. That poor guy. He got tuberculosis. He never had a chance. Angelina was a mess. I got close to her. I mean ... I helped her. I was the only one here who could. We were by his side day and night. We had to cover our mouths so as not to get the sickness. We couldn't afford a doctor. We did what we could to soothe his pain. First it's a bad cough. Then there's pain in the chest. Then he started coughing up blood. That's when we knew it was serious. He got weak, always tired. He began to lose weight, no appetite. Then he started to feel the cold. And this was in the middle of summer. Fever set in. He was sweating at night. And on and on it went. But there was no hope. Your mother knew this. All she wanted was for me to come back to Italy. But I insisted. I wrote her every day. Those letters I sent her ... I ordered her ... I was her husband ... I ordered her to come over ... to bring my children with her. But she wouldn't. She never intended to come. And I was torn. I had Peter dying ... and my wife was disobedient. What were my choices? I stayed to help a dying man. And it dragged on for a whole year, until Peter finally died. At that point I didn't even know your mother anymore. She wasn't the woman I had married. She left me by refusing to come here. By that time, I had grown fond of Angelina. I felt sorry for the loss of her husband. And one thing led to another. And so I stayed.

SILVIO is silent. He takes it all in for a moment and looks out. He does not let what he just heard affect him.

SILVIO
There's all this space here in America. Why are all the houses bunched up like this?

EDUARDO
Space is for the rich people. (*pause*) I was scared, Silvio. I know what you're thinking. Why didn't I just go back to Italy and grab your mother and my children and force them on the boat to America? (*pause*) You have to tell me what you're

thinking, son! You can't just keep everything bottled in like this. It isn't human!

SILVIO

If there's something you want to say, you just say it.

EDUARDO

I'm telling you I was scared. How do you think your uncle Peter got sick? He got sick on the ship. Coming over to America. People are crammed together on a ship, you come in contact with all sorts of people carrying all sorts of diseases and sickness. I was afraid that if I took one more trip, I could get sick. And I didn't want to die. So with your mother refusing to come here, and me wanting to stay alive, what choice did I have? Would it have been better if I had died too? I'm asking you to accept what I did. Under the circumstances I was in, I would like you to accept that what I did was human. It may have been a mistake, it may have been wrong. But I was human. (*pause*) Those eyes, those eyes ...

SILVIO

Eduardo, there is nothing I can do about my eyes. You see what you want to see.

EDUARDO

Then accept what I just told you.

SILVIO

That my mother is partly to blame?

EDUARDO

No. That I'm human.

SILVIO

I accept that.

EDUARDO

That was so long ago.

SILVIO

I always said that. (*pause*) You feel better?

EDUARDO
Yes. (*pause*) We can move forward?

SILVIO
Let's hope so. (*pause*) Eduardo. I'll tell you why I'm here. (*pause*) I'm having a difficult time getting started in Montreal.

EDUARDO
Why don't you move to Chicago? I can make it easier for you here. I would like to have you by my side. I still have some life in me.

SILVIO
I understand. But right now, I've got the process of immigration started in Canada. I have to see it through.

EDUARDO
So what is the difficulty?

SILVIO
I need help to get started. With a new baby on the way, I'm going to have three children to feed.

EDUARDO
You need money?

SILVIO
No. It's not money I want.

EDUARDO
What is it you need?

SILVIO
(*pause*) Back in Italy it's not only a family that you left, but a house and property. It's not much, but I grew up there, and my daughters were born in that house.

EDUARDO
That house goes back four generations.

SILVIO
I know. But your life is here now. Do you have any need for it?

EDUARDO

What are you asking me?

SILVIO

I'm asking you to sign over the deed to the house to me. I could sell it, and that would give me more than enough to get started in Montreal.

EDUARDO

You want the house? My house?

SILVIO

… in Italy. I never asked you for anything. But this much I'm asking. The house in Italy has no more use for you. You've done good here in Chicago. I worked the house, I kept it alive. It became my house when I got married. I'm now asking you to make me the owner. Will you help me?

EDUARDO

I'll do anything to help you. I have to discuss it with Angelina first. (*pause*) That's why you came here?

SILVIO

That's why I came here.

EDUARDO

To be entitled with the house?

SILVIO

Yes. With the sale of the house, I can get my family over to Montreal. You would be doing a great thing for us.

EDUARDO

It could make everything right?

SILVIO

If you want it to.

EDUARDO

I do, son. I do. We'll have a nice dinner for you tomorrow. A celebration of your arrival.

SILVIO

(*pause; he calls out*) Rita!

IDA and RITA enter the backyard. SILVIO grabs his suitcase.

RITA
  You all have a good evening.

SILVIO
  (*to EDUARDO*) I'll see you tomorrow.

  SILVIO and EDUARDO look at each other momentarily.

EDUARDO
  Sleep well.

SILVIO
  Rita, recite the poem again.

RITA
  (*smiles and curtseys*) San Pasquale Bailone
                    Protettore delle donne
                    Fam'aver un bel marito ...

  *RITA recites as she exits with SILVIO. EDDIE enters the yard with
  a glass of wine. He checks to see if SILVIO is gone. He looks over to
  IDA who seems a little anxious. EDUARDO is not paying attention.
  IDA moves towards EDUARDO, but EDDIE holds her back.
  ANGELINA enters the yard.*

ANGELINA
  Ida, please get dinner started. And you stop drinking.

  BOBBY enters the upper balcony and descends the stairs.

BOBBY
  When are we eating? I'm losing weight by the minute here.

IDA
  Come and help me set the table.

BOBBY
  What do you say we take Silvio for a spin later? Show him the
  town?

ANGELINA
  Robert, will you do as your wife tells you.

EDDIE

Come on, I'll fix us all a drink.

BOBBY

Friggin' A.

> *EDDIE, IDA and BOBBY exit. ANGELINA slowly approaches*
> *EDUARDO. He ignores her and makes his way towards the*
> *basement door.*

ANGELINA

Peter has come back from the grave.

EDUARDO

It's those eyes ...

ANGELINA

It was the strangest thing ... For a moment, I thought I was in
his presence. Peter has been dead for thirty-six years, and
there he was standing right in front of me.

EDUARDO

Get a hold of yourself! That medicine you take plays tricks
with your head.

ANGELINA

You saw what I saw, you can't deny it.

EDUARDO

He comes from the same blood line, that's all it is. He wants
the house and property in Italy. That's what he asked for.

ANGELINA

That's it? Nothing else? (*pause*) Good then. Finally I can
breathe again. My God that boy is intense. But he's kind. So
this is simpler than I thought. (*pause*) Eduardo, do you hear
me?

EDUARDO

I heard you, stop nagging me.

ANGELINA

Don't fight him on this. You know what they say, the living
perform the will of the dead.

EDUARDO
Stop reading those stupid newspapers! I'm not going to be
pushed around.

ANGELINA
He's asking for something that is right. Don't let your foolish
pride get in the way. We don't need him here. We have our
own children to think about. Understand?

EDUARDO
It's a lot to ask for.

ANGELINA
(*taps her cane on the ground*) This is my life you're playing with
here. I have my children to protect. One wrong move with
Silvio, and you will unleash a fury you could not have possibly
imagined. Did you see those eyes? They are the scariest things
I've ever seen. We have everything we need here. And you
don't need that house in Italy. So give him what by right should
be his anyway. He's your first-born son. Don't begrudge him
this. This will make amends in the eyes of God. He's the one
you have to watch out for.

EDUARDO
There are other ways to help him.

ANGELINA
Silvio has sparked a curiosity in our children. Curiosity leads
to questions. Questions need answers. And God forgive you if
you make the wrong move. I want this over with. He will get
what's coming to him, and let him be. That is the only way.
We're getting too old to be selfish here. That boy needs your
help. Give it to him.

EDUARDO
He didn't call me Father.

ANGELINA
What did you expect? He doesn't know you.

EDUARDO
It's a sign of respect.

ANGELINA

We don't need his respect. We need his understanding.

ANGELINA enters into the house. EDUARDO opens the basement door and slams the door shut as he exits. EDDIE enters the dining room with a glass of wine.

EDDIE

How's Dad?

ANGELINA

We don't need World War Three. Not in this house.

EDDIE

Why wasn't I told about Silvio? About his life, his service in the war?

ANGELINA

Stop being so curious.

EDDIE

I'm tired of sweeping things under the rug in this family. What's the big deal? Daddy's first marriage ended thirty-six years ago. People leave each other every day. And they move on with their lives.

ANGELINA

Silvio told you about his war experience?

EDDIE

He told me some of it. He fought in the desert. He's a war hero, Ma. Why would Daddy keep this from me? He's my brother.

ANGELINA

Why must you drink?

EDDIE

It's just a glass before dinner!

ANGELINA

Don't get cross with me.

EDDIE

Stop avoiding my questions.

ANGELINA

Now you listen to me, sonny. You want answers that are just impossible to give. I've lived my life sheltering you from your father's rage. And I will go on protecting you. The least I can get is a little appreciation for that. You think it's easy to make a life with your father? He saved my life, and I feel forever indebted and grateful to him. You can't just throw out those feelings. Now, love your brother. Love him all you want. Help him get what he wants. But then for the love of God, send him on his way. Do you understand? For your father, you must do this.

ANGELINA exits. EDDIE gulps down his wine, as the lights fade to black.

Scene Three

Later that night. IDA is on the upper balcony looking out, deep in thought. BOBBY enters onto the upper balcony.

BOBBY

You coming to bed? (*pause*) You're not going to resolve this all alone. When a father has more than one child, he has the burden of doing what's right for all of them. He can't go singling out one child and make him the favourite. Especially when he hardly knows that child.

IDA

But Silvio got the least from Daddy. He got nothing, in fact.

BOBBY

And now he's asking for everything. Look, Ida, I've seen families torn apart because of issues like this. Land and property go a long way in dividing a family unless the father makes the right decision. Now Silvio had no right coming here and asking for the land and property. That is not fair to your father, it's not fair to Eddie. And it's not fair to you.

IDA

I don't need it.

BOBBY

You say that now. What about later? Do you still want to be living up here the rest of your life?

IDA

It just doesn't seem right.

BOBBY

I'll tell you what's right, Ida. What's right is having your father disperse of what's his equally. I'm your husband and I have every right to fight for what's yours.

IDA

Before Silvio came here we never even discussed the land and property in Italy. We all assumed he just sold everything when he came to Chicago.

BOBBY

Well he didn't. And now we have to deal with it. Look. This was supposed to be a reunion between father and son. Now we know what your brother's intentions were all along. He's been invited to live here with us, so we can help him get on his way. But he doesn't want that. He wants the whole kit and caboodle. Now I think that's a little ambitious on his part.

IDA

My father left him when he was a baby. Don't you have any heart?

BOBBY

We're talking about the future here. Do you have any idea what that land and house in Italy is worth? I just got off the phone with Jerry at the shop. His father ... Mr. Lipinski, he's made a killing in real estate. He has contacts. He'll find out for us what it's all worth. My God, Ida, your father might be giving away a fortune here. And then what are we left with? Huh? Ever thought of that? You have as much right to that land as Silvio does. Now I feel bad with him growing up alone, but it looks to me like Silvio did pretty good for himself.

IDA

How do you know?

BOBBY

You see that suit he's wearing? I know an expensive suit when I see one. I've been around a little bit. I've seen the men in town who wear those suits. In the clubs. The big shots. An ordinary guy does not dress like that. You hear me talking here? We don't know a goddamned thing about your brother, and now he comes around asking for it all. It's just not right.

IDA

You said ... when we got married ... you said that in five years the shop would be yours. It's now ten, and you're still a hired mechanic.

BOBBY

I can't help it if things just didn't go my way. But do I bring home a pay cheque? Do I earn enough to get the things you want? You've never complained. I'm still young. I'll own that shop one day, and it's gonna happen sooner than you think.

IDA

How's that?

BOBBY

How long do you think old man Turdy is gonna last? With his heart condition, I give him a year, maybe two, and he'll be forced to sell it. I'm the only guy in the shop who could run it. And Turdy likes me. He'll sell me his business. And then we'll be flying. You see what I'm saying, Ida? That land in Italy could get us that shop. It's what we always dreamed of.

IDA

It's *your* dream, Bobby. Owning your own car shop has nothing to do with me. You're the one doing all the talking, Bobby. You're the one who's already made the plans. You're the one who can't make it without my family.

BOBBY

Well I'll be damned. You're my wife. I thought we were in this together? This is just fucking great. This is just ... just ... just ... fucking terrific. Man your brother has really put a spell on you. Is that what this is about? You think I'm doing some kind of usurping here? My God, woman, what's gotten into you? When I met you, you wanted to leave your family quicker than a fox can find his hole. I wanted to wait. Remember that? I wanted to give us some time before we got married so I can get myself off the ground. But you needed to leave the house. Your controlling mother ... or did we conveniently forget this? Now I got to have this shit ... my shortcomings ... rubbed in my face because I'm just trying to catch up here. You couldn't wait to get married. I had plans too, Ida. I had plans. And marriage wasn't one of them.

IDA

(*pause*) Things would've been better if we had children of our own. The focus would've been different. You think delaying our wedding plans would've made a difference? You promised me children. Remember that one? (*pause*) But we move on, don't we? We move forward in spite of the failed plans. We do that because we want to. Because we need to. And now a long lost brother has come into my life and all I ask for is a little understanding.

> *EDDIE enters the living room. He pours himself a glass of wine. He drinks.*

BOBBY

(*suddenly grabs IDA and kisses her*) There's my girl.

> *He begins to undress her. She unzips his pants. They kiss.*

C'mon.

> *He leads her inside.*
>   *EDDIE takes his glass and heads out into the backyard with the bottle. SILVIO quietly enters the backyard.*

EDDIE

Couldn't sleep?

SILVIO

It's been a long day, and still I can't sleep.

EDDIE

There's a lot on your mind.

SILVIO

I never look forward to sleeping.

EDDIE

Don't worry about the old man. He'll do the right thing and give you what's rightfully yours. He needs to do this more than you think.

SILVIO

Look, Eddie, it's not much I'm asking for. But it will secure my family.

EDDIE

You don't need to explain. I want you to have what's coming to you. No one should ever refuse the request of a war hero.

SILVIO

I'm no war hero.

EDDIE

You fought the war.

SILVIO

But I'm no hero. It was wrong.

EDDIE

The war? Hell, someone had to put a stop to it. We'd all be speaking German otherwise.

SILVIO

It's not that simple.

EDDIE

But it's over now. You're moving on. And I'll be there to help you. C'mon, drink up.

He hands SILVIO the bottle of wine.

You don't want me to drink alone, do you?

SILVIO

You're drunk.

EDDIE

I think I am.

SILVIO

(*pause*) Why are you up so late?

EDDIE

This isn't late. Besides. Hard to sleep when your father snores like a donkey.

SILVIO

He snores ...

EDDIE

You can hear him clear across to the other side of the house.

He imitates the snore.

First it's a ... (*makes the sound of the typical snore*) Then the orchestra kicks in. (*exhales accompanied by a donkey sound*) Wait ... it's not over ... then there's this ... sound of relief ... sort of like ... ahhhhh ... with another snort. Friggin' orchestra, I tell ya. Consider yourself lucky that you're staying at Rita's. You'd never get any sleep here.

SILVIO

(*laughing*) A donkey ...

EDDIE

(*laughing*) A donkey ... sometimes it's a horse.

SILVIO

A horse ...

EDDIE

Hell, it's practically a barn in there. All you need is the pigs and a few chickens, and we can start our own farm. (*laughing uncontrollably*)

They continue laughing until it finally subsides.

Man. You don't know what you're missing.

He makes the donkey sound again, and the two of them lose it in laughter once again.

I just shared my first moment of laughter with my brother at the expense of my father. We're like kids, me and you, aren't we? (*pause*) Shit. Why couldn't I have had this growing up?

SILVIO
What?

EDDIE
This ... what we're having right now. I could've used a brother
like you.

SILVIO
There's time, Eddie, there's time.

EDDIE
Fucking mothers.

SILVIO
Eddie.

EDDIE
... family, the whole thing, you try to be the good son, your
father is never happy. I wasted so much time. I just couldn't
let go of my parents, and look where it got me.

SILVIO
You have to live your life, Eddie.

EDDIE
You know the way mothers are? Especially Italian mothers. I
mean they treat us boys like babies.

SILVIO
It's not a bad thing to have parents. You will learn to appreciate
that one day.

EDDIE
It's the meddling, it's the constant judging, you can never
satisfy them. I'm just saying, it wasn't all rosy here. I know some
Irish kids, they've been on their own since they were seventeen.

SILVIO
You've been on your own.

EDDIE
Of course. I made my own way, I had my own place. Had my
own girl. And we loved each other, Silvio. We were a pair.
Couldn't keep us apart.

SILVIO

Is it your work?

EDDIE

No. My job had nothing to do with it. I just couldn't let go of my mother. When she retired, someone had to look after her.

SILVIO

Ida lives upstairs.

EDDIE

She has her own life, and Bobby doesn't make it easy. Dad puts my mom through hell. I came back to be peacemaker. I thought I'd give it one more year, you know, move back in with the folks, save some money, and then marry my girl. But she just couldn't wait. And now what do I have? Nothing.

SILVIO

Your mother means well.

EDDIE

I lost my girl, Silvio. I just wish they all could go to hell. Mother, father, the whole thing. I mean who needs it? Where does it get you?

SILVIO

Give it some time.

EDDIE

At least you didn't have to worry about your mother.

SILVIO

No. I had to be there for her. I come from another world, Eddie. Where I come from, they expect the children to take care of the parents when they get older. It's expected of us.

EDDIE

Why? She had her own life. And she wasn't alone. She moved on with her life.

SILVIO

What do you mean?

EDDIE
You had a step-father. Your mother re-married.

SILVIO
No she never did.

EDDIE
(*pause*) Yes. (*pause*) Your mother found another man. Which is why she never came to Chicago. (*pause*) She left my father for another man.

SILVIO
No, Eddie. That's not what happened. My mother never re-married. They were never divorced. The Church would never allow her to re-marry under those circumstances.

EDDIE
But, my father said there was a divorce. A mutually understood separation. My father wouldn't have re-married otherwise.

SILVIO
I'm sorry, Eddie, that's not what happened.

EDDIE
Yes that's what happened. If not it makes me a bastard child! Doesn't it?

SILVIO
No, no, no, no. Don't say that.

EDDIE
Do you understand what you're saying? What else has my father not told me?

EDDIE enters into the dining room, SILVIO follows him in.

SILVIO
Eddie. The past is the past. There is no way to undo it.

EDDIE
I need to know!

SILVIO
Eddie, don't do this. What good will it do?

EDDIE

You can't come into this house, and tell me that your mother
never re-married. If there was no formal divorce, then the
Church would not have married my father. Either that, or
he's lied to me. He never married my mother, and that makes
me a bastard. And I don't like to know that I'm a bastard.
Now what did my father do thirty-six years ago?

SILVIO

What happened back then was between my mother and your
father.

EDDIE

I am not a bastard!

SILVIO

(*grabs EDDIE, forcing him to look deep into his eyes*) Eddie, look at
me. I'm going to say this once. You are the legitimate child of
your father. He gave you his name. Now let it go. Let it go.

*A fear seems to pervade EDDIE. He's clearly drunk too much wine.
SILVIO sits EDDIE at the table.*

EDDIE

It's amazing the repercussions of a man's actions so long ago.
Why the lies? Why the secrets? What good do they do?

SILVIO

C'mon. You've had enough.

EDDIE

I'm not a bastard.

SILVIO

Sshhh …

EDDIE

I'm not …

He breaks down.

Silvio, you had to pay for my father's sins.

SILVIO
Sshhh …

EDDIE
Forgive me … Forgive me for not being there …

SILVIO
Get some sleep.

He kisses EDDIE on the head. He then moves to leave.

EDDIE
Silvio. Do you hear the donkey?

SILVIO listens for a second and then makes his way back into the yard. He takes the bottle of wine and just gulps it down. He looks out, as the lights fade slowly to black.

Silvio at four years old.

Top left: Silvio's conscription army photo, Italy, circa 1940.

Bottom left: Silvio in Belgium, circa 1955.

Top right: Silvo in Belgium, 1955.

Silvio in Chicago, 1956.

Silvio at his uncle's grave in Chicago, 1957.

ACT TWO

Scene One

The following day. Music is heard playing from a phonograph from the lower house. IDA is sitting on the bench quietly sipping wine. BOBBY runs into the yard from the lane.

BOBBY

Ida! Ida. Spoke with Turdy today. Let him know that when he's ready to sell, I'm ready to buy. Shoulda seen the relief on his face. A man likes to know that what he created will have a future. And I'm the one to give it to him. As soon as we're ready, we can talk business.

IDA

You did it. You did it for us. Thank you, Bobby.

BOBBY

I love you, baby. Did you talk to Eddie, yet?

IDA

No. Let me handle the rest. You took care of Turdy, I'll take care of my family.

BOBBY

That's good, baby, that's good. There's no stopping us now, Poopsy.

He takes her in his arms and kisses her. He starts to dance to the slow tune of the music. IDA is enjoying the moment. EDDIE enters the dining room. He drops his briefcase on the table and looks out the back door. He shakes his head and shuts off the music. He pours himself a glass of wine and enters the backyard.

IDA

(*breaks off the dancing*) Honey, why don't you go get me my sweater?

BOBBY ascends the stairs and exits.

EDDIE

When did our parents marry?

IDA

March 12, 1921. Why?

EDDIE

Have you ever seen the marriage certificate?

IDA

Why would I want to see that?

EDDIE

You and Ma talk ... you ever discuss this with her?

IDA

No. Why would we? About a marriage certificate? What kind of thing is that to talk about?

EDDIE

Ida, remember Daddy always told us how his first wife ... Silvio's mother, left him for another man? That she re-married? (*pause*) Well she never did. Silvio told me. His mother never re-married, and there never was another man.

IDA

There was a divorce.

EDDIE

No. They never divorced.

IDA

But Daddy said ...

EDDIE

Daddy said a lot of things ...

IDA
  There had to be a divorce, otherwise the Church never
  would've married them.

EDDIE
  Or he could've lied?

IDA
  To the priest? You don't lie to the priest.

EDDIE
  People lie every day to the priest.

IDA
  Why would they do that?

EDDIE
  So they can be forgiven their sins.

IDA
  By lying?

EDDIE
  Ida, a man is not going to impart to a priest his innermost sins.

IDA
  That's what confession is about. To confess your sins.

EDDIE
  And you do that by lying. You tell the truth to the doctor, and
  you lie to a priest. Silvio's mother never re-married.

  BOBBY enters the upper balcony.

BOBBY
  Honey, where's the sweater?

IDA
  Check in the closet.

BOBBY
  I did.

IDA

    Check in the living room.

BOBBY

    Playing hide-and-go-seek with a fucking sweater here!

    BOBBY exits.

IDA

    How can we know for sure?

EDDIE

    Why would Silvio make up something like that? Ida, do you
    see what I'm getting at? If our parents weren't legally married,
    that makes us a pair of bastards.

IDA

    What!

    EDUARDO enters the backyard from the alley.

EDUARDO

    Is dinner ready? Where's Silvio?

IDA

    He went to the graveyard today.

EDUARDO

    Where's my keys? Can't find my keys. Why did he go to the
    graveyard?

EDDIE

    (*opens the basement door*) He's paying his respects to a dead
    uncle.

EDUARDO

    He never knew him.

EDDIE

    What difference does it make?

EDUARDO

    Why are you always against me?

EDDIE

I'm just telling you where he is. Let's have a quiet night, okay.
Now we have to talk about the land.

EDUARDO

· That house has been in my family for four generations. The
Rosatos fought with Garibaldi.

EDDIE

I don't care if they fought with the Romans. Your life is here,
and you don't need it.

IDA

Is it worth a lot?

EDUARDO exits into the basement.

EDDIE

It doesn't matter. You do the right thing and give it to him.
Pa. Do you hear me?

IDA

Isn't that a lot to ask for?

EDDIE

Ida, we're not having this discussion right now. There's been
thirty-six years of nothing between father and son. He's not
asking for much.

*BOBBY enters the upper balcony with the sweater and descends the
stairs.*

BOBBY

(*hands IDA the sweater*) Let's have some music. (*to himself*)
Swear to God, try to get a little life into this family.

He exits into the house.

EDDIE

It's a hard thing to begin a new life in a foreign land. Nothing
wrong in helping out.

IDA

A house and property is something you inherit, you don't ask for it.

Music is heard playing from the lower house, as BOBBY re-enters the dining room and pours himself a glass of wine.

EDDIE

You listen to me good, Ida. I don't know what you're thinking. But you better drop it. This is a non-issue. Understand?

BOBBY

(*entering the yard*) Seems like this is something that should be discussed as a family, don't you think, Poopsy? First of all, Eddie, I'm part of this family whether you like it or not. What affects Ida affects me and that's all there is to it. You always get your way around here, but this is something that we are going to talk about. Land and property is something I know about. It's bigger than you think. It's bigger than a family. Why? Because it has everything in it that a family was and will ever be.

EDDIE

What the hell does that mean?

BOBBY

It means, Eddie-boy, that your father has more than one child. There's you and there's my wife here. And I'm not about to stand here and let what might be coming her way, something that could affect the future of this family, get up and walk away. You're talking about land here. You have as much claim to it as Silvio does.

EDDIE

I don't need the land.

BOBBY

You sure about that?

EDDIE

You greedy son of a bitch. I can't believe you, Ida.

IDA

Silvio just can't come into our lives like this and demand such a thing. There are other people involved here.

EDDIE

You actually convinced her of this.

IDA

I didn't need any convincing. That land is as much mine as it is Silvio's. We have to do what's right here, and what's right is sharing the land. Bobby has given me everything he's got, and it's only proper that I do my share. This should have never been raised in the first place. Silvio should've had the good will to discuss it with us first. Then we could've brought it to Daddy as a family.

EDDIE

My God, Ida! The least we can do is to rectify what Daddy did to him. Where is your common decency? How can you allow yourself to think like this? We have everything we need here. Don't make Bobby's failings in life influence your thoughts here.

BOBBY

I am not a failure!

EDUARDO enters from the basement with a prosciuto.

EDUARDO

You're nothing but a stupid fucking chooch. You can't even impregnate my daughter and give me a grandson. You stay out of this. Understand? Silvio is getting the land and that's that! I don't want to hear another word of this. Is that understood? All of you.

Exits into the house.

BOBBY

This is just … just … just … just … fucking … just … fucking great.

He takes a seat on the bench and quietly sips his wine.
They all stand, silent, as ANGELINA enters the dining room.

ANGELINA

Ida, honey, you want to set the table? (*enters the yard*) Eddie,
why don't you put on that tie I got you last summer. (*to
BOBBY*) What's with the long face? Ida, dear. This is between
your father and his son. There will be other things for you in
your future.

*BOBBY gulps down his wine and enters the house. He grabs the
bottle of wine and exits.*

You have to let these men get on with their lives. No use
standing in the middle of all this. Eddie here means well for
his brother. You should be proud that he has the good sense
of looking after the family. And right now, Silvio is the one
who needs the most. So don't get cross with your brother.
(*pause*) Eddie, why don't you go put on that tie?

EDDIE exits into the house.

Put on your good face, dear, I don't want my princess to be
all riled up about this. Me and you are gonna work on Rita
tonight and we'll get Eddie married before you know it.

IDA

Oh, Ma! Will you stop with that!

She exits into the house.

ANGELINA

Bring out the good dishes. And don't forget the wine glasses.
We don't want Silvio thinking we live like a bunch of peasants
here. (*to herself*) Dio mio, aiutami.

SILVIO and RITA enter the yard. SILVIO carries a box of pastries.

RITA

Buona sera, signora.

She kisses ANGELINA on the cheeks.

ANGELINA

Buona sera, signorina. Buona sera, Silvio.

SILVIO hands her the pastries.

Grazie. Hope you brought an appetite, we'll have a feast for
you tonight. Rita, you look so pretty. You're old enough to
settle down. Isn't that right, Silvio? (*pause*) So how did it go?

SILVIO
I'm glad I went.

ANGELINA
Your uncle ... rest his soul ... I'm sure he appreciated you
paying your respects. Paying your respects is the first act of a
decent man. And you are a decent man, Silvio. I want you to
know that. Eddie! Rita's here!

She exits into the house.

SILVIO
Rita, tell me. It's something Angelina said yesterday. When my
uncle Peter died, your parents came back to Italy. Why is that?

RITA
Eduardo drove them away. They came back here after I was
born because my father needed to work. And his only contact
with America was here in Chicago. You know, your uncle
Peter and my father were very close. He goes to the grave site
twice a year. He says there's no one here to mourn him. To
remember him. I wouldn't put too much on what Angelina
says. She hasn't been to the grave site since they buried him.
My father will tell you. The grave keeper we spoke to today,
he'll tell you. He knows everything that goes on over there.
Who goes, how often. He never once saw Angelina there. I
don't think she cares.

EDDIE enters the backyard with an empty bottle.

EDDIE
Well, good evening. Rita, I'm glad you joined us tonight. It'll
be just like the old times. The families getting together. You
know, Silvio, there was a time, when our families, hell all the
Italians, we just went from house to house. Always visiting. It
was very social. I miss that. (*pause*) Well let me get you a drink.
Rita, you in for some wine?

89

RITA

I'd love a glass.

SILVIO

Shouldn't you eat something first?

EDDIE

Let her have a glass. (*exits into the basement*)

> *IDA enters with a tablecloth and sets it on the table. BOBBY enters the dining room.*

IDA

Could you be a little more social?

> *She exits.*

BOBBY

(*enters the backyard*) Well well, if it ain't the two love birds. Any more tricks up your sleeve soldier boy?

SILVIO

Excuse me?

BOBBY

When I did my time in the army, they put me to work fixing engines and stuff. Only thing I missed was the fighting. Would've loved to put a bullet in some Kraut's head. All that trouble they started. You got to cozy up with them didn't you?

RITA

With the Germans?

BOBBY

Well, yeah. Didn't the Germans teach the Italians how to hold a gun and shoot straight? It's not like the Italians knew what they were doing. Now you're here to set things right. I mean between you and your father.

RITA

Bobby, you should stop sniffing gasoline. Not good for the brain.

BOBBY

Why don't you go give Ida a hand setting the table? You don't expect my wife to do all the work now, do you?

EDDIE

(*enters the backyard with a bottle of wine*) Nobody brought you glasses?

RITA

I'll go.

She exits into the house.

BOBBY

You know what the shortest book ever written is? *Italian War Heroes.* (*laughs*) Get it. Italian Fucking War Heroes. (*pause*) You and your brother here. Your half-brother. Is that what you are to him, Silvio? A half-brother. Man that sounds incomplete doesn't it. Hey, Silvio, we played this game in the army.

BOBBY stands toe to toe with SILVIO.

Now you lock eyes with me.

SILVIO holds his position as BOBBY taunts him.

We'll see who blinks first.

BOBBY suddenly takes a swing at SILVIO but his fist stops not an inch from SILVIO's face. SILVIO does not even blink. EDDIE is alarmed at what he's just seen.

Wow. They trained you right. Didn't even blink an eye.

EDUARDO enters the backyard.

EDUARDO

Buona sera, Silvio.

SILVIO

Buona sera.

RITA enters the backyard with glasses. She hands one each to the men. EDUARDO takes the bottle and pours the wine. They clink glasses.

EDUARDO

After dinner maybe we can take a walk. Facciamo 'na passegiatta. Nobody walks anymore. In Italy we used to take these walks after dinner. Come back for coffee. I'm still a man from the old country, with his old ways. Your presence here reminds me of how much I miss the old country. It's in my blood. It will always be a part of me. Salute. To our health and family.

They drink.

Rita, how about you?

He pours her a glass.

That's a girl. How do you like my wine?

SILVIO

It's very good. Where do you get the grapes?

EDUARDO

They come from California. Not like the Italian grapes, but it's getting there.

EDDIE

You make your own wine, Silvio?

SILVIO

The first thing I'm going to do when I settle in is make me a wine press.

EDDIE

You can make a wine press?

EDUARDO

They know how to make everything back home. It's not like here. People have skills over there.

BOBBY

Not like here eh, Pa?

EDUARDO

You kids have everything made for you. How are you going to learn anything?

BOBBY
Well I'll be damned. You're living in the most productive,
powerful, advanced country in the world, and you don't think
we know how to make anything?

ANGELINA enters the backyard.

ANGELINA
Why don't you all come on in? Eddie, did you ask Rita for a
date? You two should be on the couch talking alone.

EDUARDO
There she goes putting her head in people's business.

BOBBY
She's right, Eddie. It ain't right her hanging around Silvio
here. I'm just saying, you know, they start hanging around,
people start talking. I mean, Rita is a pretty girl, you're the
stranger coming to town sweeping people off their feet.

ANGELINA
Ma che dice stu coccialone! So, Rita, how about Saturday?
You free Saturday?

EDDIE
I'm busy Saturday. I'll be out of town. I'll be in Springfield for
business.

ANGELINA
Springfield? That's two hundred miles away. That's a long
distance just to make a sale.

*IDA enters the dining room with the plates and cutlery and begins
to set the table.*

IDA
(*shouting*) I threw the pasta in! Dinner will be ready in about
ten minutes!

EDDIE
How long do you think it'll be before you settle in permanently?

SILVIO

I need to establish my base first. Get a job, a house. When I have that, I'll call over the rest of my family.

ANGELINA

Isn't it cold up in Canada?

EDDIE

Not any colder than here, Ma.

ANGELINA

But it's so north. And then with all those horses running around.

SILVIO

The cold is the least of my problems. Once I'm settled in, my wife and children will keep me warm. My mother.

EDUARDO

Your mother?

SILVIO

My plan is to bring over everybody. My wife, children and my mother.

EDUARDO

Your mother? You didn't tell me this.

IDA

(*opens the back door*) Why don't we take our seats? Rita, you want to help me?

EDUARDO

Why didn't you tell me you were bringing your mother? I don't like surprises. You should've told me this.

SILVIO

I just assumed when I said my family it included my mother.

EDUARDO

You're bringing your mother ... I can't believe this ...

SILVIO

You don't expect me to just leave her there.

BOBBY

Oooh. Who would've thought soldier boy is also a mama's boy.

RITA

Leave him alone.

BOBBY

Get out of my way, girl.

He shoves her aside.

SILVIO

(*calmly*) Don't touch her like that.

BOBBY

Or what?

SILVIO

Or nothing. I'm just telling you once.

BOBBY

It's nothing, Silvio. I'm just making a little conversational discourse here.

SILVIO

That's fine. You can talk to me all you want. Just don't touch her like that.

BOBBY

Well, well. He's got a temper.

IDA

(*enters the backyard*) Bobby. Come inside, please! Can we all come inside.

SILVIO

Ma is getting old. I can't leave her alone.

EDUARDO

She will make her way to America. Your mother has no business being here.

SILVIO

I'm not going to live here.

ANGELINA

Eduardo, come inside. We'll discuss this tomorrow.

EDUARDO

Will you stay out of this!

RITA

Silvio, I think we should leave.

EDUARDO

(*to ANGELINA*) Filomena can't come here, she just can't.

BOBBY

(*overlapping*) I've had it with your shit!

EDDIE

Will you shut up!

RITA

C'mon, Silvio ...

BOBBY

Get out of the fucking way!

*RITA reaches out for SILVIO, but BOBBY shoves her aside with a little
more force. He then turns to punch SILVIO with the full intention of
landing one this time. SILVIO, with lightning speed, fends off the
attack and grabs BOBBY by the throat and puts a chokehold on
him. SILVIO lays him up against the basement door. Everyone is
stunned. There is silence except for BOBBY gasping for air.*

SILVIO

There is only one way to get out of this, Bobby. You answer this
one question. Don't worry now, you have enough air to get you
to the question. You want to live, or you want to die? I've killed
before. I can do it again. So you answer the question. Live or
die? You seeing a light now, Bobby? A light inside my eyes?
That's the light that goes out depending on how you answer
the question. You want to live, just blink your eyes.

*BOBBY does so. SILVIO keeps the hold for a few more seconds, and
then lets him go.*

IDA

My God ...

>   *She runs to BOBBY's side.*
>   *BOBBY is coughing and gasping for air to the point of vomiting.*
>   *It's manic and pathetic. Clearly humiliated he climbs up the*
>   *stairway coughing and gasping all the way. He opens the back*
>   *door and exits. IDA turns to face SILVIO. She slaps him in the*
>   *face, and exits up the stairs.*

ANGELINA

You end this right now, you hear me? Give him what he wants
and let it go. Dio aiutaci!

>   *She exits into the house.*

EDUARDO

Porco dio! What kind of trouble are you trying to start here,
son?

EDDIE

Bobby had no right to start this. He has no right to anything.

EDUARDO

You're right. This is no business of Bobby's. I'm glad you
taught that kid a lesson. I should've done it myself. Now you
can come on in and we'll have our dinner. We can put this
aside. Tomorrow we can start fresh once again. You're going
to come here and I'll give you what you have coming to you. I
think two hundred dollars should do it.

EDDIE

What? What are you talking about?

EDUARDO

The land is a complicated piece of business. I'll give you two
hundred dollars, that should be enough to get what you want.

SILVIO

I don't want your money.

EDUARDO

Well you're going to get it.

SILVIO
I didn't ask for money.

EDUARDO
This is the way it's going to be. I'm giving you money. I've said my piece.

He exits into the house.

EDDIE
Pa, that's not what we discussed. Pa! Pa! Silvio, I can rectify this ... let me ... just hold on ...

He exits into the house.

RITA
Your father ... I warned you about him ... your father ...

She weeps.

SILVIO
He's not my father ... I never had one ... There, there now ... angels don't cry ... angels don't cry.

The lights fade slowly to black.

Scene Two

Late morning, the next day. IDA is on the upper balcony looking out. RITA comes running into the backyard. IDA descends the stairs.

IDA
Did you find him?

RITA
No.

IDA
Where could he be?

RITA
I don't know, I checked all over.

IDA

What happened? We heard the screaming.

RITA

It was a terrible night, Ida. The scariest thing I've ever been through.

IDA

The screams?

RITA

The nightmare ... oh my God ... Ida ... it was awful. We heard the screaming coming from Silvio's room. It woke up my father. I was scared ... didn't know what to do ... so my father opened the door to his room. And then we saw ... what we saw ... he ... oh my God ...

IDA

Rita, calm down, and just take a breath. What happened?

RITA

He kept shouting, "God forgive me. God forgive me. Father in Heaven, forgive my sins." And then he'd stop like he was listening to someone. He ... he ... just fell silent for a second. And then it began all over again. My father had enough at this point and approached him. Silvio leaped back lightning quick. It was instant reflex. Like his body is conditioned to defend itself. Regardless of what his mind says. And then he started to rub his leg, when he finally came out of it. I tell you, Ida, for that minute, I swear I saw a battlefield. A desert. And death.

IDA

The memories.

RITA

They don't go away. (*pause*) When he came to, he just hugged my father and mother, and apologized. He eventually went to sleep from sheer exhaustion. This morning when we got up, his suitcase was packed and lying on the bed. And he was gone.

IDA

Eddie's out looking for him.

RITA

Your father must be reasonable about this. Silvio needs
attention, and he needs to be taken care of.

IDA

You have to get over this now. My brother is a married man. He
has children. You mustn't think of him that way.

RITA

What way? What are you insinuating?

IDA

You know what I'm talking about. Your feelings for him are
not in the proper place. You're practically related, for God's
sake!

RITA

I don't think of him that way, Ida. How can you say this to me?

IDA

You idolize him! You worship the ground he walks on.
Anyone can see it.

RITA

Why are you saying these things? He's like a brother to me. I
love him like a brother. There's nothing else ... Shame on
you! You and your whole family are poisoned with despicable
willful acts of ruthless inhuman conduct! Your father has
poisoned all of you!

IDA slaps RITA in the face. RITA slaps her back.

How dare you! (*pause*) You just don't see it do you? None of
you see it. It's not about the land. It's not about the house
and property. None of you here can see that what Silvio is
asking for is deeper than a few measly metres of land. And a
house. He is seeking something deeper. He wants some sort
of validation from his father. For his life. For what he went
through. That maybe in spite of it all, being given the land is
proof of your father's acceptance of him. Don't you see that?
Can't you see beyond the dollars and cents?

IDA is silenced by this. BOBBY enters the upper balcony with a baseball bat and the boy suit.

BOBBY

You go on now, girl. You're not welcome here anymore.

RITA

Come down here. I have something to show you.

BOBBY

He's hiding somewhere, I just know it. Jump out unexpectedly. You go ahead, Silvio! I'm ready this time. (*flings the suit to the ground*) And you can take this back! I don't need no shit rubbed in my face!

IDA picks up the suit and places it on the patio table.

RITA

Will you shut up and come down. He's not here.

BOBBY

I don't care, Rita. I'll come down, but I'll start swinging if I have to. Now I have a right to defend myself in my home. I could kill him, and I'll be protected because the Constitution of the United States says so. I have the right to defend my homestead. You hear that, Silvio! I'm not putting up with your bullshit anymore! Now, Rita, you take a real close look.

BOBBY reveals a gun placed inside his pants at the waist.

I'm not shitting you now. This is the real thing. I have that right. And there's nothing anyone can do about it. Now go on.

IDA

Will you put that away.

BOBBY

Go on now, girl. I ain't putting up with this. I won't be pushed around by a Fascist.

RITA

(*makes her way up the stairs*) I want to show you something.

BOBBY

I'm warning you, little girl. This is none of your business.

RITA

What, are you gonna shoot me? Look, either you come down, or I'm coming up. Which is it gonna be?

BOBBY

He's not hiding?

IDA

He's not here!

BOBBY

Go on down, now.

RITA makes her way down again.

You just keep your distance, there's no telling how I'll react if he comes in.

He makes his way down the stairs.

Where is he anyway? What the hell was all that shouting last night? Crying over some spilt milk. Fuck that shit! Eduardo is doing the right thing. Giving him some money is the way to settle all this. Now if Silvio was smart he'll take what's coming his way and call it a day.

RITA

Did you ever see the land and property Eduardo left in Italy?

BOBBY

My eyes can't see that far, Rita. But I have someone making inquiries about its worth. I'm no idiot. People hit the jackpot when it comes to land and property. Ever heard of "forty acres and a mule"?

RITA

Yes.

BOBBY

Okay. Well that's what Lincoln gave the slaves after the Civil War. Some of them prospered because of that. They were just given a huge lot of land so they can move on with their lives. Now I think that was a pretty good deal.

RITA

Most of that land was reclaimed by the former owners after Lincoln died. The Negroes didn't get anything in the end.

BOBBY

I don't know what you're talking about. Forty acres and a mule was part of government policy. They knew that land would settle the issue.

RITA

It didn't. What's the matter with you?

BOBBY

No point in getting cross with me, Rita. I'm just stating a fact. Land is the oldest issue in the book. And no one has the right to come in here and just ask for it.

RITA

You are such an idiot.

BOBBY

You watch your mouth, little girl, because I'm not taking this anymore.

IDA

You said you had something to show him. What is it?

RITA takes out a few photographs and hands them to BOBBY.

BOBBY

Who are these kids?

RITA

Those are Silvio's children. Look at the surroundings. That's the house on the inside. This is the land that surrounds it. Look at it.

BOBBY

You can't tell from a photograph. The perspective on this is all off.

IDA
(*looking at the photos*) This is it?

RITA
That's it. That's what this argument is all about.

BOBBY
You cannot tell the size of a property based on a ... dis-perspective photograph.

RITA
Look at the size of these kids in relation to the house. Now look at them in relation to the land. This is the backyard. It's a little garden and a work area.

BOBBY
This can't be right.

RITA
Look in the corner there. What is that?

BOBBY
Looks like a beer barrel.

RITA
It's a wine barrel. Silvio makes his own wine. You know the size of a barrel. Have you ever seen one? Look at the space it takes up. What are you left with?

BOBBY
This ... this ... I can't believe it. You could fit this whole property into the backyard here. And that includes the house. We can't be talking more than ...

He begins to laugh hysterically.

This is insane! You're talking about, at most, a couple of thousand dollars here. It's net worth. I mean ... this is a chicken coop! This is what Silvio wants?

His laughing is uncontrollable.

We were fighting here over a piece of land the size of a fucking chicken coop!

IDA

This is what Silvio wants? This is the Rosato home? Silvio grew up in this little thing. My God, I can't believe this.

BOBBY continues laughing as IDA collects the photographs and hands them back to RITA.

BOBBY

Ida, can you imagine making love in there? "Now move over, son, while I screw your mother here." (*laughs*) "Wait, Daddy, I gotta look the other way before you do it." "Now wait a minute, son, you know there's no room to look the other way, you're gonna have to just shut your eyes now, while me and Mommy do the goody in bed here."

IDA

You're disgusting.

BOBBY

(*laughs*) Well if I haven't seen it all now. (*eventually his laughing subsides*) Well that settles the issue. Your father should just give Silvio what he wants and then they can move on with their lives. Forty acres and a mule ... this is twenty feet and a barrel. I'm going to work. This family can drive you crazy ...

EDDIE enters the backyard carrying a briefcase. He seems oblivious to everyone and makes his way to the back door. He stops. Turns back.

EDDIE

Looked all over ... the bars ... the relatives ... the church, even went to the graveyard. Where's Daddy?

IDA

He and Ma went to the bank to withdraw some money for Silvio.

BOBBY

Two hundred dollars. That should last Silvio about a month.

EDDIE

Money is not what he asked for.

BOBBY

Hey, I'm on your side, buddy. Eduardo should give him the land and call it a day.

EDDIE

Really? (*notices the baseball bat*) Where you going?

BOBBY

I'm going to work. I'm done talking about a whole lot of nothing.

EDDIE

(*to RITA*) You okay?

RITA

I'm fine. I just want Silvio back home. He's endured enough.

EDDIE

I know that. I'm going to make things right.

IDA

Why did you go to the church?

EDDIE

That's between me and Pa.

He enters the dining room. Pours himself a glass of wine.

BOBBY

What does the church have to do with all this?

IDA

No use in getting the church involved. (*enters the dining room*) Eddie, please. Let Daddy have his peace, and let it go.

BOBBY and RITA gather by the back door to listen.

EDDIE

We have to make things right by Silvio. What have we done with our lives, Ida? There's a greater goal here: to do what's right for an entire family. He's our brother. We must correct the mistakes of our parents, or we're just a pair of lost souls pretending to be human. Deliberate inaction when you have the power to set it right is the biggest crime of all. Silvio's life is a lived life. Ours was sheltered by lies and deceit.

IDA

What lies are you talking about? Eddie, please.

EDUARDO and ANGELINA enter the backyard.

EDUARDO

Where's Silvio?

EDDIE steps into the backyard. IDA follows him out.

EDDIE

You can't just throw him some money and think it'll resolve everything.

ANGELINA

Why don't you all go to work and leave your father be.

EDUARDO

He intends to sell the land anyway. It all comes down to money.

EDDIE

You think two hundred dollars will make up for thirty-six years of neglect?

ANGELINA

Do not speak to your father in that tone.

EDUARDO

You're drunk.

EDDIE

In vino veritas. Why don't we all pour down some truth serum and so we can really talk about this.

ANGELINA

Eddie, basta! Please!

EDDIE

You were set on giving Silvio the land until he mentioned he was bringing his mother here. And then you had a change of heart and decided to give him some measly dollars instead. Why is that?

107

EDUARDO

I want to share my land and property with all my children. It's only fair.

EDDIE

(*to IDA*) Do you want the land?

IDA

Eddie ...

EDDIE

Just answer the question!

IDA

No.

EDDIE

(*to BOBBY*) Do you need the land?

BOBBY

Hell no.

EDDIE

There you go, Pa. Your children have spoken. We don't want it, we don't need it. Just give it to Silvio and it settles everything.

EDUARDO

Bastardo! You think you can speak to me that way in my home? You need the land for your future, son. How do you expect to get started in life?

BOBBY

What the hell you talking about?

He takes the photographs from RITA.

This is it, Pa. This can't be worth more than a couple of thousand dollars. At most. I know a little something about land, and this ain't nothing.

EDUARDO

Where did you get these?

He grabs the photographs.

BOBBY looks over towards RITA.

You here to start some trouble, Rita? Va via! You take these and get out of here.

EDDIE

You stay right there, Rita. We're gonna have this long awaited talk right now, and we're gonna resolve this. You think two hundred dollars will settle the issue? You're setting him up to fail. You want him to fail so he'll be forced back to Italy with his mother and we'll never hear of them again. Why are you so afraid of Silvio bringing over his mother?

EDUARDO

I'm not afraid of her.

EDDIE

Good then. Give Silvio the land. He can make enough money to get all his family over including his mother. Now do the right thing.

EDUARDO

Why are you doing this?

EDDIE

I want you to hear this, sis. When were you married? And when you married my mother here, was that before or after your divorce from Filomena? Your first wife? Silvio's mother.

EDUARDO

I know who she is!

EDDIE

Am I a bastard, Pa? Am I a bastard son? Am I?

EDUARDO

Why you little …

He goes for him, but BOBBY steps in the way.

BOBBY

Whoa whoa whoa, there now, Pa. Take it easy.

EDUARDO

You have no right to talk to me like that! Porco cane!

EDDIE

I have every right to know who I am!

BOBBY

You listen up, Eddie. You go to the bathroom there and splash some water on your face. You're gonna have to calm down.

EDDIE

Shut up! (*regains his composure*) I went out looking for my brother this morning. I looked all over until I came across the church. Went in and spoke to Father Antonio. Told him there was a land issue within the family. Gonna need my dad's marriage certificate. Got it right here in my briefcase. (*pause*) How do you do it, Pa? How can you be so remorseless? What are you afraid of? When Silvio comes here, I want you to look him in the eyes and tell him that you are going to give him two hundred dollars. Two hundred measly American dollars, and that will decide what he's worth. You tell him that. And then I want you to look me in the eyes and tell me that I am not a bastard.

IDA

Did you divorce your first wife? (*pause*) Did you divorce your first wife? Silvio's mother never re-married. You told us that she did. That she left you. Was there a divorce?

EDUARDO

(*pause*) No.

IDA

So you lied to the Church?

ANGELINA

Ida, dear, those were difficult times.

IDA

Did you lie to the Church? Father Antonio who married me and Bobby. The one we confess our sins to. Did you lie to him?

EDUARDO

(*pause*) Yes.

IDA

What you did is illegal. I know something about the law, and the law does not allow a man to have two wives.

ANGELINA

Your father saved my life. I was ready to throw myself into the lake. My life was over, until your father saved me. He made a choice that made possible everything we have here today.

IDA

You had two children back in Italy.

EDUARDO

I had no life there.

IDA

You had two children!

ANGELINA

Ida, please stop this. (*to EDUARDO*) Just give Silvio the land and let's get on with our lives.

EDUARDO

I will not give him the land! He's out for revenge! Him and his mother, for what I've done. And I'm not gonna have it. Helping my son is one thing, but Filomena, that's something else. I know her. She despised all of my ambitions, my plans. And now she wants to come here to get her revenge.

EDDIE

She's not coming here. Silvio is moving to Montreal.

EDUARDO

Now, he says that. Once he's settled in, he'll want to come to America. And then his mother will throw me in jail. Now is that what you want, son?

EDDIE

Silvio is not out for revenge.

EDUARDO

How do you know that? That boy has anger in him, there's no telling what he'll do. Now everyone here ... you listen to me ... I made mistakes in the past, but it's not worth going to jail over. I was just trying to survive. I'm tired of walking these streets with all the paisans talking behind my back. I won't have that.

SILVIO enters the backyard carrying his suitcase. RITA runs to him. His presence catches everybody off-guard. BOBBY keeps his distance.

RITA

Silvio. Are you okay? Where were you?

SILVIO

I'm fine. I went to the train station to buy a ticket home. I just said good-bye to your parents. I picked up my bag, and I came over here to say my good-byes.

He notices the suit on the patio table.

EDUARDO enters into the dining room and sits at the table.

Eddie, can you call me a taxi, please. There's a lot of work to do. Not a minute to waste. Angelina, ti voglio ingraziare. Spero che la tua salute va meglio. Grazie molto per la tua conoscenza.

He kisses her on both cheeks.

Perdonami per i miei comportamenti ieri.

ANGELINA

Non ti preoccupare. Basta che ti sei calmato.

SILVIO

Bobby ...

BOBBY

You stay right there, Silvio.

SILVIO

(*takes out his hand to shake*) I'm sorry for what I did to you last night. Please accept my apologies. That wasn't me.

BOBBY
Who the hell was it?

SILVIO
Please. Forgive me.

BOBBY
(*shows SILVIO the gun*) We got witnesses here.

IDA
Will you put that away!

BOBBY lays the gun down.

SILVIO
Please. (*shakes BOBBY's hand*) Ida. I'm sorry we didn't have
more time ... but I was honoured to know you ... to finally
meet you.

He kisses her on both cheeks.

IDA
Silvio, you can't leave like this.

SILVIO
I never intended to cause any harm here. My visit here was
meant to be peaceful. I apologize to you from the bottom of
my heart. I just wish we could've met under different
circumstances. Eddie ... Eddie ... take care of your family,
they're counting on you.

EDDIE
Silvio, please. Let's make things right. You can't just go off
like this.

SILVIO
Eddie ... Eddie, my brother. My brother ... you come visit me
sometime. We'll catch up. We'll be the brothers we were
meant to be.

Pause. SILVIO steps into the dining room.

Eduardo.

113

EDUARDO
You can't leave on an empty stomach. Have some lunch.

SILVIO
No, thank you.

EDUARDO
You don't want to eat in my house?

SILVIO
I should go.

EDUARDO
I have something for you. ·

SILVIO
No. No. I asked for too much. It was wrong. It was very forth-coming of me. Very selfish. You have other children to think about. One should never ask for such things from a desperate point. I wasn't thinking. And I apologize.

SILVIO steps back out into the backyard.

I want you all here to know, as God is my judge, that I will not pursue anymore the property or the land.

EDUARDO steps out into the backyard.

So, Eduardo, I want to say good-bye. (*takes out his hand*)

The two men look at each other. EDUARDO does not shake SILVIO's hand.

EDUARDO
Sit down. Have a coffee. Ida, make some coffee.

SILVIO
No, I really … Eddie if you can call me a taxi …

EDUARDO
You can at least give your father the satisfaction of having a coffee with you.

SILVIO
Please, there's no reason to prolong this …

EDUARDO

You have to go, go. No point in forcing you.

SILVIO

Eduardo, it's best for everyone ...

EDUARDO

Call me Father.

SILVIO

(*pause*) Good-bye.

The phone rings. IDA gets it.

IDA

(*on phone*) Hello ... hello ... I don't understand ... yes ... the
Rosato home. Yes ... who? He's here ... (*to SILVIO*) Silvio, wait!
It's for you. It's long distance, from Italy.

SILVIO

(*steps into the house and takes the phone*) Pronto. Si. E Silvio.
Non ti sento. Parla piu alto. Si. Pronto. (*pause*) Fammi parlare
a Carmela. Carmela? Pronto. Carmela, ti voglio bene. Si. Si.
(*pause*) Maschio? (*cries*) E un maschio. (*pause*) Grazie,
Carmela. Grazie, ti voglio tanto tanto bene. Ci vedremo fra
poco. Si. Un gran baccione. Salutami a mama. Pronto. Ma?
Ma, sto bene. Si. Tutto bene. Ma ... Ma ... ti voglio bene.
Ciao. Fammi parlare a Maria. Maria? E papa. Stai attento a
mama. Mi ascolta? Papa ti vo tanto bene. Maria ... Maria ...
mi ascolta ... stai attento all' piccolino. Ciao, ciao.

He hangs up. He crosses to RITA.

My wife gave birth. It's a boy. I have a son.

RITA

Auguro.

EDDIE

Way to go, Silvio!

He hugs him.

This is a cause for celebration!

115

IDA

Congratulations, Silvio.

ANGELINA

Auguro.

SILVIO

Thank you. Thank you all. Grazie.

He regains his composure.

There's lots of work to do now. I have my boy.

EDUARDO

You have your son. You're gonna need this now.

He takes out an envelope.

Son, this is no time to be proud. Take the money. How do you expect to feed three kids? You asked for help. I'm giving it to you.

SILVIO

I didn't ask for money.

EDUARDO

What difference does it make? This is help.

He removes the money from the envelope.

Here. Look at it. Take it.

SILVIO

(*pause*) No.

EDUARDO

You son of a bitch! What do you think you're doing?

SILVIO

Eddie, will you please call me a taxi.

EDUARDO

You're not going anywhere. You're not going anywhere, son, until you accept my money. Who do you think you are, refusing me?

ANGELINA

Your father is trying to help you. Why won't you take it? You have no idea the sacrifices this man has made in his life to give us all a life here. No idea. You've brought division and unrest to my family. Now the least you can do is to accept your father's offer of life. Yes, Silvio. Life. You think you're gonna have an easy time of it? A wife ... three kids ... in a strange land ... you need his help.

BOBBY

God damn, Silvio! Just take it!

RITA

(*picks up SILVIO's suitcase*) Let's go. We've had enough.

EDDIE

Wait. Silvio. You stay right there. (*to EDUARDO*) Are you going to abandon him a second time? What is the matter with you? How can you be so heartless?

EDUARDO

(*slaps EDDIE across the face*) I've heard enough from you. Now go inside and sober up!

EDDIE

I've seen it all now. I've seen it all. The problem, Daddy, is that not everyone else here has seen it. And that includes Silvio. He might have some doubt in him as to the truth of his parents' actions so long ago. Well, my brother, let me clarify it for you. So that once and for all, you will have no doubt as to who your mother is, and who your father is. Daddy, I asked you a question before. When were you married? (*pause*) You won't answer? I'll just check the marriage certificate here, which Father Antonio was so kind to give me.

He takes out the marriage certificate from his briefcase.

Ever seen one, Ida? This is what it looks like.

EDUARDO

Put that away.

EDDIE

Oh no, Daddy. This puts it all to rest.

EDUARDO

I'm ordering you to put that away.

EDDIE

You have no right to order me! None! No right to tell me what is right or what is wrong. You see, Ida. We never really knew when our parents got married. This here paper tells it all. Look at it.

ANGELINA

Eddie, my son, please don't do this.

IDA

What's your point, Eddie?

EDDIE

My point, Ida, is that they were married ... look here ... May 14, 1921. Do you see that? May 14, 1921. Not March 12. When were you born? When did Peter die? Now do the math. I went to the graveyard. The date is on the gravestone. It's all there for everybody to see.

BOBBY

I don't understand.

EDDIE

It means, Bobby, that my mother here was pregnant before her first husband ... Peter died. Do the math. You were carrying on an affair with this man while your first husband was dying. Was dying! You couldn't even wait for the man to die! (*pause*) So there you go, Silvio. You can leave now knowing that your mother did nothing wrong. All she did was to wait for a man to whom she promised to live a life with. And your father, your non-father here cared for no one but himself.

IDA

How could you?

EDUARDO

Ida, please, you have to understand ...

118

IDA

No. Don't touch me. What kind of man are you? You sorry
pathetic old man! Have you no heart? Have you no heart?

ANGELINA

This is more than anyone should bear.

SILVIO and RITA begin to exit.

EDUARDO

(*to SILVIO*) We're not done here. I'm not going to have my life
spat on like this. (*to EDDIE*) Keep reading, son. The marriage
certificate ... don't just look at the dates, look at the signatures.
Go ahead, look. I needed two witnesses to confirm my status
with the Church. Who do you think vouched for me? Who?

He turns to RITA.

Your parents, little girl. Your father and your mother did the
lying for me.

RITA

No they didn't!

EDUARDO

Yes they did. Look at the document. You'll see their signatures.
I needed two witnesses to tell the priest that I wasn't married.
And your parents lied on my behalf.

RITA

No! They couldn't! They wouldn't do that to Silvio!

EDUARDO

They could and they did!

RITA

No, that's not true ... you pathetic monster ... it's not true ...
Silvio ... it can't be ... it can't be! You cold-hearted bastard! I
hate you! I hate you!

SILVIO crosses to RITA to comfort her.

He's the devil ... this man is possessed ... he's the devil
himself. You must go away from this place. Silvio ... please ...

EDUARDO

What are you gonna do, Silvio? Condemn everybody because of their past? None of you understand what I did! None of you! Sacrifices were made. I made them. To make a life. No one can understand that until you've lived it. You have no right to base decisions on actions from the past. But I want you all to know that sacrifices were made, and they will be respected. Now you take this money, son, you take it. And there will be more coming. I'm offering you a chance for a new beginning. Take the money.

SILVIO

I don't want your money.

EDUARDO

If you go like this, you go, and don't ever come back here again.

SILVIO moves to leave.

You ungrateful bastard! You disgraceful son of a whore!

This stops SILVIO dead in his tracks. He's calm, eerily calm. He's heard enough and they all know it. He crosses into the house with deadly efficiency and calm and dials the phone.

SILVIO

(*on phone*) Taxi please. 475 Crescent Road. I'm going to the train station. About twenty minutes.

Hangs up. Crosses into the backyard.

You think what you did in your life was a sacrifice? To whom? For what? You talk of sacrifices like you have a claim on it. Eddie here was right. Getting to know the truth. That's the only way. And I'm tired of you and your twisted lies. I came here in search of a father. I didn't find one. But you go on like you have been a father to me all along.

RITA

Silvio …

SILVIO

It's okay, Rita. This man will not go to his death without knowing what he did.

EDUARDO
I have nothing to apologize for! Nothing! You came here
knowing exactly what you wanted to do. Your mother
probably set you up to this. After all these years you want
revenge, well you're not going to have it! And I have nothing
to apologize for!

SILVIO
That's right. That's right. You have nothing to apologize for.

EDUARDO
I made the sacrifices!

SILVIO
What sacrifices? Tell me, which ones? (*picks up the suit*)
Remember this? This is the only contact I ever had with you.
You sent it after your parents begged you to help your
children. This is what I got. A suit. What did you think a suit
was going to do? Suddenly make things right? But the child
who wore this was hopeful. Oh, yes he was. That's why he hung
on to it. Thinking that one day his father was going to come
back and make things right. If not with his wife, then at least
for his children. Time passed, and soon the child was a young
man. And that hope turned to despair. That's when the child
in the man died. It died. You killed a little boy's hopes and
dreams. A little boy does not have to die to be considered dead,
but when you take away his dreams, that may be worse. Still the
child survived because of the kindness and generosity of friends
in the village. And they helped because they felt sorry for us.
Do you know what it's like to be surrounded by pity your whole
life? But the people in the village came through, because they
refused to have a family amongst them die. They took it upon
themselves to help in whatever way they could. Which is why
you are forever shamed back home. You asked me when I got
here what they think about you. You disgraced the name. They
look upon you with scorn. You have no dignity. You are not
even considered a man. Because what you did was the greatest
of sins. The deliberate abandonment of his family. You think a
suit was going to make up for all that? A suit!

He throws the suit at EDUARDO.

121

BOBBY
Easy there now, Silvio.

SILVIO
I'm not done yet.

IDA
We understand, Silvio. We understand your pain.

SILVIO
What pain! What pain! What do you know about pain?

EDUARDO
I've heard enough.

SILVIO
No you haven't! You haven't heard anything yet. You talk
about sacrifices. All the waiting that little boy did after he got
the suit. The wait for salvation. You know where he found it?
In his mother. His mother! The one you just called a whore! I
never once saw her shed a tear. Not once. Until I heard her
crying one night as we were sleeping. I pretended not to
notice. So that she could have her pride. You know when she
cried? I'll tell you exactly when. It was October 16, 1940. That
was the day I got my draft notice. And that was the day my
mother cried. And didn't my mother beg your parents to get
in touch with you to get me out of there? Out of the war. Out
of Mussolini's war. Out of harm's way. And didn't your father
send you a telegram, countless letters, begging you to get me
out of there by bringing me here to America? But those
letters went unanswered. Do you know what silence is like?
You could cut it in half, and still it's just as silent. What would
it have taken to send for your son? What? Do you call that a
sacrifice? Do you? This is your father, Eddie. Look at him.
Ida, this is the man you call Daddy.

EDUARDO
You're blaming me for the war now?

SILVIO

I'm blaming you for the silence! You put a son on the earth, and you had a duty to look after him until he was big enough to fend for himself.

EDUARDO

You want us to feel sorry for you? Is that what this is about?

SILVIO

No. I'm done with pity. It's a useless emotion. I just don't understand why, since I got here, you expected me to call you Father.

EDUARDO

Because I am your father and you will respect me as such! You want to cut me down in front of everyone here. My family. You came here to destroy me.

SILVIO

You destroyed yourself. I had nothing to do with it. All I wanted was a little piece of land that would've ensured the future of my family including my mother. But you can't stand the fact that we survived. We survived in spite of your silence.

EDUARDO

There, you survived. Now you can go!

IDA

How can you speak to him like that?

EDUARDO

Look what he's doing to me! He wanted to do this all along. You think it was easy here? You think I didn't have my own problems here?

IDA

What problems?

EDUARDO

You're taking his side now?

IDA

Just stop with the lies!

EDUARDO

What lies? I can't be blamed for all this! I can't be blamed for the war! You spent the better part of it in a war camp. You want to come here like you're some fucking hero!

SILVIO

You son of a bitch! You ugly stupid fucking cadaver! You think my time there was a vacation?

His rage is uncontrollable.

You want to make light of my actions!

EDUARDO

I could've helped you if ... if ...

SILVIO

IF WHAT! IF WHAT!

Everyone is taken aback as SILVIO is transported back to his horror.

THERE'S BLOOD ON MY HANDS! AND THERE'S BLOOD ON YOUR SOUL! You think the war was a game?

He picks up BOBBY's gun.
Everyone is now completely stunned. He moves towards EDUARDO with the gun.

Ever been fired at? Huh? You know what it's like? Well do you? You know what it's like to be under orders? Ever fired a machine gun? Huh? Ordered to open fire!

SILVIO fires the gun.

Again! (*fires*) Again! (*fires*) Again! (*fires*) Again!

He fires. Now he points the gun to his head.

You know what it's like to have a gun pointed at your head? Do you?

He removes the gun away from his head and fires.

Again, and again! You know what it's like to have a piece of metal rip right through your leg? DO YOU!

RITA crosses to SILVIO and disarms him gently. RITA throws the gun away. This seems to calm SILVIO down.

I refused to die. What kept me alive was the burning desire to live so I can face my real enemy ... You, and tell you to your face, what your actions caused. I thought no. I cannot die. I will not die. My war is still not finished. I have to finish this in Chicago one day.

IDA is openly weeping. BOBBY goes to her side. RITA is holding back her tears. Everyone else is shocked by what they just heard. SILVIO is exhausted now, and takes a seat. EDDIE crosses to SILVIO and puts his arm around him. EDUARDO throws the envelope to the ground and exits into the house.

IDA
Daddy ... Daddy ... you can't leave like this! Daddy! I'm talking to you! Daddy!

She turns to ANGELINA.

Mother. He can't leave like this.

ANGELINA looks over to SILVIO and then just walks away into the house.

Mother! Mother! What's wrong with you people? You can't leave like this.

BOBBY
Baby ... baby ... sshhh ... they can't hear you ... it's okay ... give them their space ... it's okay ...

A car honking is heard from the front of the house.

That must be the taxi. I'll tell him to wait.

He exits the yard.

IDA
(*hugs SILVIO*) I'm sorry ... I'm so so sorry. I just want you to know that ... that ... I didn't know ... you have to believe me.

SILVIO hugs her back.

EDDIE

Silvio. My brother. I want you to know that if you come to live in Chicago, I could make it easier for you. I can help you. Please reconsider.

SILVIO

I can't live here. Not in the same city. My life will be in Montreal. That's where I'll be. You can come visit any time.

EDDIE

But what if you can't make a go of it?

SILVIO

I will. I have a boy of my own now. He needs to know that he has a father. And my little girls, I won't let them down. I can't let them down. They need a fighting chance in this life. So you don't worry about me. I'll be okay. Because I'm going to give them that chance.

EDDIE

Silvio …

SILVIO

Eddie … Do you think a foreign land like Canada will scare me? Not a chance.

BOBBY re-enters the yard.

BOBBY

He'll wait a few minutes. For what it's worth, I just want to say, we didn't know any of this. But you have time, Silvio, to make things right for yourself. (*pause*) You take care, now.

He shakes SILVIO's hand.

EDDIE

Silvio, I need you now. I need you … I need you so badly now …

SILVIO

Eddie. I won't be that far. We don't have to make distance a reason not to see each other. Come on, now. Courage. You can do it …

EDDIE

    (*hugs his brother and kisses him on the cheeks*) We'll let you two be ...

SILVIO

    Eddie. (*pause*) Thank you.

    EDDIE, IDA and BOBBY exit into the house. SILVIO and RITA look at each other. It's very difficult for them to say good-bye.

    Rita. If you get tired of living here, just remember you have a home with me. Understand? When you finish your studies, you're going to come visit me and my family in Montreal. And we'll have a feast for you. I'll always be there for you.

RITA

    Silvio ... (*weeping*)

SILVIO

    You make peace with this. Understand? Don't let it eat you up inside. I love your parents. I love them very much. There now. Come on. Forza. Are you an Italian?

RITA

    ... yes ...

SILVIO

    Then come on. If you keep crying you're going to wet all your wings here.

RITA

    Wings?

SILVIO

    You're an angel, aren't you? How do you expect to fly?

RITA

    Oh, Silvio ... I'll miss you so much ...

SILVIO

    (*hugs her*) You've brought so much joy to my life. Thank you. Thank you.

    He stops himself from getting more emotional and grabs his suitcase.

Now you keep reading. And you keep writing. Because it's
the one with knowledge that pulls ahead. And always. Always.
Your head up. Understand? Good-bye.

He kisses her on the cheeks, and then hugs her one last time.

Good-bye.

RITA
Good-bye.

*SILVIO gives her one last look and then leaves by the front, the
same way he came in at the beginning. He takes one last look
towards RITA and then he's gone.*

Good-bye.

*RITA begins to compose herself. She picks up the little boy's suit
from the ground and folds it neatly. She brings it to her face and
hugs it.*
    The lights fade slowly to black.

THE END.